A NEW CULTURE OF LEARNING
CULTIVATING THE IMAGINATION FOR A WORLD OF CONSTANT CHANGE

Douglas Thomas and
John Seely Brown

Funded by
MISSION COLLEGE
Carl D. Perkins Vocational and Technical Education Act Grant

We dedicate this book to the parents of children who are growing up in the digital age. We hope our contribution will illuminate the strange and wondrous learning styles of the next generation.

—DT and JSB

PRAISE FOR A NEW CULTURE OF LEARNING

"*A New Culture of Learning* is at once simple, subtle, and sophisticated. Douglas Thomas and John Seely Brown help us understand the profound changes brought about by digital technology in a way that calms anxieties and fires hope for the future. We come to understand that the twenty-first century is about embracing change. It is about how concepts like tacit knowledge, indwelling, and collective play can restore America's competitive edge. The new culture of learning draws energy from massive information networks while honoring the bounded and structured environments in which experimentation unleashes powerful imaginations.

This is not a book about school reform but rather an exploration of how people of all ages are learning by doing, asking fresh questions, and working together to solve problems and seize opportunities. It is a call to action to reconceive how we learn at all ages. This is a profoundly optimistic book that gives us the confidence to embrace change—indeed, it compels us to celebrate change as it guides us toward the future."

—*Jonathan Fanton, former president of the John D. and Catherine T. MacArthur Foundation*

"Thomas and Brown introduce the provocative and extremely important new paradigm of a 'culture of learning,' which is appropriate for a world characterized by continual change, ubiquitous connectivity, and almost unlimited access to knowledge resources. Drawing upon their extensive experience with digital technology, learning environments, and new social structures, such as massively multiplayer online gaming, the authors make a strong case for reframing learning as a social experience more akin to play, relying on experiment and imagination to cultivate learning collectives as the natural successors to current paradigms used in today's schools. This is a MUST READ for anyone interested in the future of education."

—*James J. Duderstadt, President Emeritus, University of Michigan and author of* A UNIVERSITY FOR THE 21ST CENTURY

"*A New Culture of Learning* may provide for the digital media and learning movement what Thomas Paine's *Common Sense* did for the colonists during the American Revolution—a straightforward, direct explanation of what we are fighting for and what we are fighting against. Douglas Thomas and John Seely Brown lay out a step-by-step argument for why learning is changing in the twenty-first century and what schools need to do to accommodate the resulting new practices. Using vivid narratives of people, institutions, and practices at the heart of the changes, and drawing from a growing body of literature outlining new pedagogical paradigms, the authors place the terms of the argument in language that is accessible to lay readers. You can give this book to the educator in your life who wants to become an agent of change. My hope is that our schools will soon embrace Thomas and Brown's emphasis on knowing, making, and playing."

—Henry Jenkins, Provost's Professor of Communication, Journalism, and Cinematic Arts, University of Southern California, and the author of CONFRONTING THE CHALLENGES OF A PARTICIPATORY CULTURE: MEDIA EDUCATION FOR THE 21ST CENTURY

"*A New Culture of Learning* is at once persuasive and optimistic—a combination that is all too rare but which flows directly from its authors' insights about learning in the digital age. Smart teachers have always known that students learn from each other, and we have been admonished from time immemorial to learn from our mistakes. Thomas and Brown show that access to ubiquitous information, and the ability to communicate and collaborate with groups large and small at low cost, can create powerful learning environments that evolve as quickly as knowledge itself.

Pearls of wisdom leap from almost every page: 'Blogs are a medium for learning, but they do not teach'; 'We know more than we can say.' The old saw that 'people learn in different ways' becomes the insight that different people, presented with the same information in the same way, will learn different things. Hence, they can learn a great deal from each other: 'Play becomes a strategy for embracing change, rather than a way for growing out of it.'

My advice to teachers at all levels is to use this book to create learning environments that harness the intelligence and eagerness of today's students. Thomas and Brown show us that the constant change that is so often decried as an impossible challenge for teaching in the twenty-first century is actually an asset to be deployed in the service of learning."

—*Paul Courant, University Librarian and Dean of Libraries, Harold T. Shapiro Collegiate Professor of Public Policy, Arthur F. Thurnau Professor of Economics and Information, and former Provost, University of Michigan*

"Douglas Thomas and John Seely Brown portray the new world of learning gracefully, vividly, and convincingly."

—*Howard Gardner, John H. and Elisabeth A. Hobbs Professor of Cognition and Education, Harvard Graduate School of Education*

"At the start of this remarkable book, Douglas Thomas and John Seely Brown pose a direct question: What happens to learning as we move from the comparative stability of the twentieth century to a more fluid and dynamic new century, where technological innovation is inciting almost constant change? The answer, if we as a society are wise enough to grasp it, is a promising and powerful new culture of learning. This new environment is made possible by the emergence of massively networked information and our ability to inhabit it and experiment within its secure borders.

A New Culture of Learning provides a sturdy theoretical framework as well as many compelling, accessible stories that serve as guides to the future that the authors envision.

The tenets of this new culture of learning include access to almost limitless information through digital media, play as a strategy for embracing complexity and change, learning proceeding from active engagement with the world, peer-to-peer interaction and communities of like-minded learners enriching learning, and questions being more valuable than answers.

American education is at a crossroads. Given the relentless pace of change, doing nothing is tantamount to sliding backwards. By illuminating how play helps to transform both information networks and experimentation, and how collective inquiry unleashes the power of imagination, *A New Culture of Learning* provides an irresistible path to the future. Let us hope that we have the wisdom to follow."

—*Joel Myerson, Director, Forum for the Future of Higher Education*

"Thomas and Brown bring to life their idea of 'collectives,' or self-reinforcing communities of mentors and learners, by describing the new learning environments that exist in massively multiplayer online games—and this is nothing short of a brilliant revelation to those of us who have been hesitant to see the value of gaming in education. A mind-bending, and ultimately optimistic, look at the future of education, the book is filled with so many brilliant ideas that I immediately read it through a second time."

—*Steve Hargadon, Founder, Classroom 2.0*

"Among the most emotional and politically charged debates in this country is the state of education. Sides are sharply drawn with critics demanding change—but change to what? Into this debate step Douglas Thomas and John Seely Brown, two highly thoughtful people who have listened, observed, and played with ideas that have led them to a completely new and considered approach, one that needs to be heard by all citizens. They present not an 'either-or' approach but a 'both-and' set of ideas that reframe the discussion about what is core—learning. Learning that takes place everywhere and continuously. Learning that happens when we are open to it, and in unexpected circumstances. Thomas and Brown's ideas will open minds and help us get beyond the arguments that are holding back our ability to see and understand what is already happening in front of our eyes—the forces of learning in the twenty-first century that will make a difference in our lives—if we can embrace the possibilities of a new culture of learning."

—*Richard P. O'Neill, President, Highlands Group*

"*A New Culture of Learning* is an important book that upends the assumption that teaching is necessary for learning to occur and replaces that long-held but false belief with a powerful and convincing argument for the role of structured play, questioning, and imagination in peer-to-peer collectives. Thomas and Brown's concise and compelling narrative, replete with playful tales from the digital frontier, is essential reading for educators, policymakers, and all others concerned with the future of our children."

—*Beth Simone Noveck, Professor of Law, New York Law School; Director, Information Law and Policy; and author of* WIKI GOVERNMENT: HOW TECHNOLOGY CAN MAKE GOVERNMENT BETTER, DEMOCRACY STRONGER, AND CITIZENS MORE POWERFUL

"Douglas Thomas and John Seely Brown have written an inspiring resource for any parent, teacher, or other adult who cares about kids and the future they will build for us all. *A New Culture of Learning* shows all the ways that games, virtual environments, social networks, and other forms of digital culture offer possibilities for imaginative play, which helps kids deal with the challenges of today's monumental technological and social changes. Instead of wringing their hands over the supposed ills our children face from the Internet, Thomas and Brown applaud the ways kids learn through their imaginative interactions online. Thomas and Brown are the John Dewey of the digital age."

—*Cathy N. Davidson, Ruth F. DeVarney Professor of English and John Hope Franklin Humanities Institute Professor of Interdisciplinary Studies, Duke University*

"Douglas Thomas and John Seely Brown make it clear that education is too often a mechanistic, solo activity delivered to the young. It doesn't have to be that way—learning can be a messy, social, playful, embedded, constant activity. We would do well, as individuals and as a culture, to listen to their message."

—*Clay Shirky, author of* COGNITIVE SURPLUS: CREATIVITY AND GENEROSITY IN A CONNECTED AGE

"Like the best games, this story-infused book compels you to explore, discover, challenge, and focus on what's most important: nonstop learning and evolution. Thomas and Brown demonstrate that collective play is not mere preparation for life, it *is* life. In order to thrive in a world of constant change, we must challenge the very nature of how we participate with one another and how we prepare for whatever comes next. Brilliant. Insightful. Revolutionary."

—*Marcia Conner, coauthor of* THE NEW SOCIAL LEARNING: A GUIDE TO TRANSFORMING ORGANIZATIONS THROUGH SOCIAL MEDIA

"Our top-down approach to learning is ineffective in the face of the information tsunami, complexity, and accelerating rates of change. Douglas Thomas and John Seely Brown describe a fresh and compelling view for the twenty-first century. They point out that learning from others is neither new nor revolutionary; it has just been ignored by most of our educational institutions. William Butler Yeats said that education is not filling a bucket but lighting a fire. *A New Culture of Learning* ignites the fire of learning how to learn. If you care about the sustainability of human progress, read this book. You'll never think about learning in the same old way again."

—*Jay Cross, Principal, Internet Time Alliance, and author of* INFORMAL LEARNING: REDISCOVERING THE NATURAL PATHWAYS THAT INSPIRE INNOVATION AND PERFORMANCE

"Thomas and Brown provide insights for engaging in the new learning paradigms all around us, which are indeed unique, nontraditional, and something that all leaders need to understand.

—*Stephen Gillett, CIO, Starbucks*

"Anyone who fears, as I do, that today's public schools are dangerously close to being irrelevant MUST read this book. The authors' argument, that questions are more important than answers, provides a road map—and a lifeline—showing how schools can prosper under the most difficult conditions. Learning is no longer static and discrete but continuous, because answers to real questions lead inevitably to more questions. This hopeful message is also a welcome departure from all the school bashing.

—*John Merrow, Education Correspondent, PBS NewsHour and President, Learning Matters*

"We need a new mode of thinking, learning, and doing—about everything from renewable energy to renewable health, pollution to poverty, global economics to global water. Douglas Thomas and John Seely Brown empower us with ways to boost our imaginations and let us harness change in the world and in ourselves. Their powerful insights give us the escape velocity to get past old learning debates and get on to using our minds collectively to conceive and invent an awesome future."

—*Tara Lemmey, CEO, Lens Ventures*

"As an 'informal learner' myself, I particularly appreciate the framework that *A New Culture of Learning* provides. If it had been around when I was still in school, I might not have dropped out. This book is essential reading not just for educators but for anyone who hopes to thrive in the twenty-first century."

—*Joichi Ito, Chairman and CEO of Creative Commons*

"*A New Culture of Learning* should be read by everyone who cares about innovation and the next generation. The work transcends the current education debate and puts forward a bold vision of lifelong learning. To inspire the next wave of entrepreneurs and change agents, we must transform our education system. This book is a great start."

—*Jack D. Hidary, cofounder, Vista Research and Chairman, National Lab Network*

TABLE OF CONTENTS

Making Change Visible

Learning Through Play and Imagination

4

LEARNING IN THE COLLECTIVE

Peer-to-Peer Learning

The Emergence of the Collective

Learning in the Collective

5

THE PERSONAL WITH THE COLLECTIVE

The New Collective

Seeing in the Dark

Collectives and Education

The Birth of the Blog

Why He Blogs

Taking the Easy Way Out

Concerted Cultivation

Collectives in the Arc of Life

6

WE KNOW MORE THAN WE CAN SAY

Tacit Learning

From Teaching to Learning

Inquiry

Questions and Answers

Learning as Inquiry

Indwelling

Dispositions and the New Culture of Learning

Collective Indwelling

1
ARC-OF-LIFE LEARNING

When people think about learning, they usually think about schools. And when people think about schools, they usually think about teachers. In this book, we take a different approach. In our view, the kind of learning that will define the twenty-first century is not taking place in a classroom—at least not in today's classroom. Rather, it is happening all around us, everywhere, and it is powerful. We call this phenomenon the *new culture of learning,* and it is grounded in a very simple question: What happens to learning when we move from the stable infrastructure of the twentieth century to the fluid infrastructure of the twenty-first century, where technology is constantly creating and responding to change? The answer is surprisingly simple.

Ironically, the relentless pace of change that is responsible for our disequilibrium is also our greatest hope. A growing digital, networked infrastructure is amplifying our ability to access and use nearly unlimited resources and incredible instruments while connecting with one another at the same time. However, the type of learning that is going on as a result looks so different from the kinds of learning described by most educational theorists that it is essentially invisible.

This new type of learning is a cultural phenomenon that underlies a large number of people's experiences and affects them in myriad ways. It takes place without books, without teachers, and without classrooms, and it requires environments that are bounded yet provide complete freedom of action within those boundaries. This familiar dynamic, in fact, structures all our contemporary notions of play, games, and imagination. Play can be defined as the tension between the rules of the game and the freedom to act within those rules. But when play happens within a medium for learning—much like a culture in a petri dish—it creates a context in which information, ideas, and passions grow. Potent tools for this type of learning already exist in the world around us and have become part of our daily lives—think of Wikipedia, Facebook, YouTube, and online games, to name just a few.

The new culture of learning allows us to recognize, harness, and institutionalize these ideas. It also requires a shift in our thinking about education. Although much of the new learning takes place outside traditional educational forums, we do not argue that classrooms are obsolete or that teaching no longer matters. Our goal is quite the opposite. We believe that this new culture of learning can augment learning in nearly every facet of education and every stage of life. It is a core part of what we think of as "arc of life" learning, which comprises the activities in our daily lives that keep us learning, growing, and exploring.

Play, questioning, and—perhaps most important—

imagination lie at the very heart of arc-of-life learning. Children, for instance, embrace play as a central part of how they experience the world, and they learn that questioning the world is one of the key ways they can understand it. Think of how a child's imagination blossoms when she discovers the "why?" game, for instance. No matter what answer an adult provides, it can always be met with the question "why?"—and the game can continue. For a child, the potential for fun is limitless. The principles of questioning and play can serve to define arc-of-life learning, and they have a tremendous effect on, and resonance with, learning today.

So what frameworks do we need to make sense of learning in our world of constant change? The new culture of learning actually comprises two elements. The first is a massive information network that provides almost unlimited access and resources to learn about anything. The second is a bounded and structured environment that allows for unlimited agency to build and experiment with things within those boundaries. The reason we have failed to embrace these notions is that neither one alone makes for effective learning. It is the combination of the two, and the interplay between them, that makes the new culture of learning so powerful.

One of the metaphors we adopt to describe this process is *cultivation*. A farmer, for example, takes the nearly unlimited resources of sunlight, wind, water, earth, and biology and consolidates them into the bounded and structured environment of a garden or farm. We see the new culture of learning as a similar kind of process—but cultivating minds instead of plants.

The stories we provide in the following pages show how the new culture of learning is intricately woven into the fabric of our society; indeed, it permeates nearly everything we do. They also illustrate how the tools for learning in this new environment make the old way of learning and schooling seem much less effective. In each case we find that the very things that are speeding up the rate of change in the world are also giving us those new tools. The trick is to figure out how to harness these new resources, which make play, questioning, and imagination the bedrocks of our new culture of learning. The question is: In the twenty-first century, how do we cultivate the *imagination?*

SAM'S STORY

Sam is nine years old. Like most kids his age, he is already familiar with the Internet. But Sam has started playing with some new software, programs like Gamestar Mechanic[1] and Scratch, which are designed to help children understand the basics of design. Gamestar Mechanic is focused on game design elements, while Scratch deals more with the fundamentals of programming.

Scratch was created at MIT as a platform to help kids gain a level of technological fluency. Its colored and coded building blocks allow a programmer to drag and drop various algorithms and procedures into a window and then link them together in different sequences to create programs. The results are immediately visible in a second window on the screen. Within a few minutes of playing with the software, kids can create basic animations and user interactions and can add their own images and backgrounds to the program.

One of Sam's first programs was an animation in which he created an avatar, using his own picture, inside a virtual Grand Canyon. The goal of the game was to move the avatar around the Grand Canyon, chasing a piece of paper that was blowing in the wind. Every time the avatar touched the paper, the player gained points.

Like many other kids, Sam quickly discovered how to program movement and how to import images for avatars and backgrounds. He also took a summer class to help him better learn how to create Scratch programs.

If we were talking about traditional approaches to learning, this would simply be a nice story, and this is probably where it would end. There is no doubt that Sam knows more about programming now than he did before and that he is able to use the tool to create something that is both interesting and personally expressive.

But Scratch has an additional element that takes the experience to a different level: a *collective,* a community of similarly minded people who helped Sam learn and meet the very particular set of needs that he had. When Sam posted his game online to that community, it became accessible to thousands of other kids who were also working with Scratch, and that's when some very interesting things started to happen. The other players were able not only to play Sam's game, but also, with the click of a button, to download it into the Scratch interface, see the code, and modify it if they wished.

Perhaps the most important aspect of all, however, was the users' ability to comment on projects they liked by clicking a "Love it?" button. What Sam found when he joined the online community was that he was no longer simply creating animations or games; he was part of a larger conversation. He was excited about receiving his first comment, of course. But when we asked Sam what it meant to be a good member of the Scratch community, we were surprised by his answer. It had nothing to do with building games or posting animations. Instead, Sam told us that the single most important thing was to "not be mean" in your comments and to make sure that you commented on something good when you came across it, as well. The game does not just teach programming; it cultivates citizenship.

One of the options that Scratch provides is to "remix" other people's work. When Sam came across a program he particularly liked, for example, he left a comment to which the original programmer responded "Wanna remix?" This invitation started a conversation between the two players. They began looking at each other's programs, changing them, modifying them, and building on them. Because anyone can download the code to any posted program and make changes to it, Scratch has a built-in system that tags any remixed content as "based on" the original programmer's content. This sense of remix has served to define a significant part of the Scratch culture.

When we asked Sam what makes a remix different from a copy, he told us without hesitation that for something to be a contribution, you have to change "three big things." It wasn't enough to make minor adjustments, such as "changing sprite movement from 14x, 3y to 15x, 4y." It required something that reflected real work done by the programmer. The goal of remixing, he told us, is to improve the program. "You get it as good as possible first," he told us, and then "if it needs improvement, you are happy to have others remix."

Sam has taken classes on Scratch that have helped him "learn a little," and he talks with two friends who use the program (though they are not part of the online community). Those interactions, however, are rarely about programming techniques. His friends are most interested in "what my comments were and who commented on me."

Yet Sam made perhaps the most revealing comment, one that tells us the most about the new culture of learning, when we asked him what he looks for in other people's programs. He told us, "something really cool you could never know yourself." While playing Scratch, Sam has learned a lot about programming and a lot about participating in online communities. But what he has learned most of all is how to learn from others.

TEACHING IN A GALAXY FAR, FAR AWAY

In the spring of 2004, one of us, Douglas Thomas, taught a course titled "Massively Multiplayer Online Games and the University of Southern California." The class met once a week for three hours and was scheduled as a seminar to be divided into three parts. Part one was lecture: Doug would go over that week's course readings, which covered some pretty heavy theoretical terrain—books and scholarly articles on game theory, identity, gender and politics, social theory, and technological determinism. Just to make sure no one questioned the course's academic rigor, he even made the intrepid undergraduates wade through not one but *two* essays by Martin Heidegger.

Each class featured a lecture for the first hour and a half, followed by forty-five minutes of discussion, and then a half hour of show-and-tell, where the students, who had previously spent time playing in the virtual world of *Star Wars Galaxies,* would share examples from their gaming experience that would illustrate course concepts.

That was the plan, at least. During the second week, the discussion time was cut short by the students' insistence that they show their examples as part of the discussion. They argued that it was the only way they could really talk about what was happening in the game world without actually being there.

By the third week, students were arriving early to class, waiting to plead their case. "Professor, I know we need to do the lecture and discussion, but we were all in the game last night and found the perfect example for class today, so can we please start with it and then do the lecture after?" Doug agreed, though he couldn't help feeling that his class was now slipping away from him. In one sense that was true. But he had missed a far more important message: Students were getting together, outside of class, and discussing how they might make the class itself better. "This just doesn't happen," Doug recalls. "At least not to me."

By the fifth week, show-and-tell lasted for two-and-a-half hours and was followed by Doug's brief attempt to make a few points about the week's readings and see if there were any questions.

By week nine, one of the students was getting married (for the third time) within the construct of the game. The entire class was invited. It was elaborate, with all sorts of in-game items repurposed to transform a guildhall into a wedding chapel. Players all helped carry candles, and the ceremony lasted over an hour.

By week ten, Doug had written off the class as an interesting experiment that, while fun for the students, was a complete failure. He complained repeatedly to his spouse (also a professor) that he was teaching them nothing and that his "teaching in a virtual world" experiment was probably something that needed to be rethought. At the very least, he decided, he needed to figure out how to regain control of his classroom.

And then Doug read the students' final exams. Every single paper was filled with examples from the students' own experiences in the game woven together with readings that had never been addressed in class, either through lecture or discussion. And the students weren't just repeating theory or quoting from source material, either—the examples were very rich and highly textured. They referenced Donna Haraway, Langdon Winner, Sherry Turkle, and, yes, even Martin Heidegger.

Far more important, however, the students referenced each other. For them, classroom time had become the least significant part of the overall experience. They had formed their own learning community and used course readings and material to make sense of what they were doing. And they had done it by themselves, for themselves.

After the course was over, Doug saw one of the students on campus and told him that he was very impressed by the quality of everyone's exams. Perhaps inappropriately, he expressed some surprise at that result. The student, however, just smiled and asked, somewhat incredulously, "What, did you think we were just playing games all semester?"

In a sense, Doug had indeed taught the students nothing. They, however, had taught him a great deal about what the new culture of learning might look like and how powerful it can be when students see each other as resources and figure out how to learn from one another.

GOOGLING THE ERROR

In northern California, Allen runs a small business writing computer code as a freelance hacker. He is fluent in nearly all the core languages and can program for a wide variety of tasks. He also has no formal training in computer programming beyond a degree in computer science he achieved nearly 50 years ago.

Allen's skill was developed in two ways: first, by experimenting with various computer language programs and compilers and second, by making mistakes. The second part would prove to be the most instructive but not for the reason one might think. Computer code provides almost endless flexibility in design, naming conventions, and routines—so much so that programmers are expected to document their code in plain language within the program to help others decipher their algorithms. But as anyone who has spent even a small amount of time around computers knows, when you run into a problem, the first thing the computer does is give you an error message. That message provides information that is often very specific to the language, program, or computer, but it is almost always completely incomprehensible and therefore useless. In some cases it can be indecipherable to even the most seasoned computer-programming veterans.

Allen took this failure and turned it into a learning opportunity. As he was learning to write code, he would write his program and run it. When it crashed, as it usually did, he would copy the obscure error code that popped up and paste it into Google. Within seconds, the search engine would present a list of discussions, FAQs, blog posts, and manual pages all citing or referring to that precise error. He learned incredible amounts of information, including the dos and don'ts of using particular aspects of code for different problems.

By "googling" the error, he was able to tap into—and learn from—large, diverse networks of programmers and hobbyists who all faced similar issues, and he often found solutions that would allow him to complete his project. Ultimately, Allen mastered every computer language he needed to start and run his own business—without ever attending a single class on programming.

GAMING ACROSS GENERATIONS

Becky and Nick are hard-core gamers. The two have been gaming together for more than a decade, going back to some of the earliest massively multiplayer online (MMO) games, such as *Ultima Online* (released in 1996) and *Dark Age of Camelot* (2001). In *World of Warcraft*, they take on the characters of a priest and a hunter, respectively. Becky describes herself as "less twitchy" than many of her team, or "guild," mates, meaning she relies less on fast reflexes than she does on patience, careful strategy, and knowledge of the game. Ambitious and risk-taking, Nick is the class leader for his guild and knows just about everything there is to know about playing a hunter in *World of Warcraft*. They have very different playing styles and attitudes toward the game, but both are core members of the guild's "raiding" culture, in which they battle fictional monsters. As part of the large group of players who are considered the best in the guild, they spend 15 to 20 hours a week taking on some of the most complex and difficult challenges that the game has to offer.

Becky also happens to be Nick's mom.

Becky and Nick are part of the increasingly common phenomenon of children, parents, and even grandparents playing online games together. In some families, the relationship is very casual; they might all play the same game, but they won't necessarily interact much. In others, playing the game together becomes the basis for family interaction. One family whose members are geographically dispersed, for example, uses the game as a way to stay in touch. Every Friday, three generations get together in *World of Warcraft's* Azeroth to play for four or five hours. Prior to that, their interactions had been limited to real-world holiday visits and periodic phone calls. Now, the children are staying home on a Friday night to spend time online with their grandparents.

We are seeing more and more intergenerational gaming, which picks up on the deeply social nature of online games while simultaneously providing a context in which even young children can play the role of "expert" in an increasingly acceptable fashion. During the time they spend together, family members are not just idly chatting; they are actively engaged with one another—questing, learning, and building teams to complete real tasks. They feel that the connections they build in the context of gaming can be about something concrete: accomplishments and shared experiences that bring them together and motivate them. Playing side by side, they also appreciate the different phases of life represented within the group and recognize each individual's distinct motivations and skill sets. What's more, everyone has fun at the same time.

CLICK HERE TO START LEARNING

Tom was 41 when he was diagnosed with adult-onset diabetes. At the hospital, he was shown a video, given several booklets and pamphlets with information about diet and treatment, and then sent home with instructions to follow up with regular visits to his physician. Each follow-up visit consisted of a brief discussion with his doctor and a blood test. A week after that, he would receive a letter in the mail with the test results and a reminder to schedule another follow-up appointment.

During this time, Tom was also visiting a website called Diabetes Daily, where he found articles about the condition written by members of the community and message forums covering topics ranging from evaluations of blood-sugar testing kits to recipes for low-sugar, low-carbohydrate meals. The site also has a live chat room, usually populated by ten to 15 people at any given time. "The chat room was really important for me right after I was diagnosed," Tom told us. "I was scared, and I didn't really know how my diabetes was going to change my life. Just seeing a bunch of people living with it, doing fine, going about their lives was a huge relief. I remember thinking if these people are doing OK, because some of them were much worse off than I was, that I was going to be fine, too."

Diabetes Daily is more than just a repository of informational resources, however. It is a community made up of thousands of people who visit the site every day to share their experiences, insights, successes, failures, and, on occasion, tragedies. For Tom, the site (along with a handful of others) started out as a place where he could go to better understand his disease. But it quickly became more than that: He found that the stories people told and the advice they gave were much more useful than the information provided by the hospital's pamphlets—so much so that he keeps up with the forums even now. He also found that all his questions had already been asked, and most had generated long series of responses. Perhaps the most important thing he found was that almost every aspect of diabetes—from diagnosis to treatment to the very standards used to measure it—was in dispute.

The forums are not intended to substitute for visits to the doctor, and dispensing medical advice is strictly prohibited. (In fact, the forum rule against doing so is listed, in bold, as the first and most important of them all. Posts that cross the line are immediately reported to forum moderators and deleted.) The forums did help Tom make sense of his visits to his doctor, however, and they provided information that wasn't available from medical professionals. "The boards give you information that doctors just can't, either because they don't know it or don't have time to tell you about it," he said. "You also learn from other people's experiences. You find out what are the right questions to ask your doctor and you can learn how to tell a good doctor from a bad one." Through the postings, Tom realized that his own doctor was truly exceptional: "More than anything," he said, "I learned how good my doctor was, especially in comparison to some of the others that are out there."

In the forums, Tom found support among fellow diabetics. From them, he learned about daily practices for managing his disease, including how to deal with others. Doctors may provide medical advice, but online communities provide much-needed social advice. "Having diabetes is very different from living with diabetes," Tom said, "and the forums are all about living with it."

Almost all the learning that occurs on the site is the result of member interaction, and it fills in the gaps in people's understanding about every aspect of the disease, from the most important to the most trivial. Perhaps the best summary of the site appears on the first page, which prominently features a small box that reads: "Newly diagnosed? Click here to start learning!"

Of particular interest to Tom was the question of how to handle pushy relatives around the holidays. "One of my online friends had posted a message about Thanksgiving. They had talked about the difference between saying 'I can't' and 'I don't' when you are offered food. Whenever you tell someone you 'can't' eat something, they tend to push you, saying 'come on, it's Thanksgiving' or 'just one bite can't hurt.' But when you tell them 'I don't eat that' it is much harder for them to say 'yes, you do.'"

THE MORAL OF THE STORIES

Each of these stories illustrates how the new culture of learning is taking root and transforming the way we think about information, imagination, and play. They also reveal many motivations for learning across generations, platforms, purposes, and goals. We can see that learning is taking place in day-to-day life through the fusion of vast informational resources with very personal, specific needs and actions. The new culture of learning gives us the freedom to make the general personal and then share our personal experience in a way that, in turn, adds to the general flow of knowledge.

The people in these stories learned much more than facts, figures, and data. They shared their interests, developed their passions, and engaged in a play of imagination. They learned to participate and experiment. In that sense, something larger was always being addressed, built, created, and cultivated. Each of these stories is about a bridge between two worlds—one that is largely public and information-based (a software program, a university, a search engine, a game, a website) and another that is intensely personal and structured (colleagues, a classroom, a business, family, the daily challenges of living with a chronic disease). The bridge between them—and what makes the concept of the new culture of learning so potent—is how the imagination was cultivated to harness the power of almost unlimited informational resources and create something personally meaningful. In each case, fusing a vast informational resource with a deeply personal motivation led to an unexpected, unplanned, or innovative use of the space. In short, the connection between resources and personal motivation led people to cultivate their imaginations and recreate the space in a new way.

Through Scratch, Sam was able to join a larger learning community and become fluent in it with time, experience, and practice. What mattered most to him were not the programs he wrote or the games he played, but his engagement with others. Even though Sam had taken classes in Scratch, the real learning took place through comments, remixing, and looking at how other people solved problems. Sam was able to draw upon a vast set of resources, to ask questions, and to build on others' work, as they built on his. In the Scratch community, everyone learns from one another.

The same kind of community emerged around *Star Wars Galaxies* for the college students. They turned to one another to understand their experiences and the course material and to make the whole thing relevant to their lives. They started to see the difference between learning and being taught. Perhaps equally important, so did their professor.

By pasting confounding error messages into Google, Allen was able to tap into—and learn from—the vast wealth of knowledge available in the global community of computer practitioners.

Emerging new platforms offer a glimpse of what might be possible for families who game together.

And in online medical communities, people use networks to build learning communities that fill the gaps in and around information about health, medicine, diet, and exercise. Those communities provide patients with the tools to ask better questions of their doctors and to make better decisions about their medical care.

In the new culture we describe, learning thus becomes a lifelong interest that is renewed and redefined on a continual basis. Furthermore, everything—and everyone—around us can be seen as resources for learning. To harness that new kind of learning and understand where we are now headed, we must dig deeply into that emerging culture. And in order to do that, we need to clarify what we mean by "culture."

2
A TALE OF
TWO CULTURES

For most of the twentieth century our educational system has been built on the assumption that teaching is necessary for learning to occur. Accordingly, education has been seen as a process of transferring information from a higher authority (the teacher) down to the student. This model, however, just can't keep up with the rapid rate of change in the twenty-first century. It's time to shift our thinking from the old model of teaching to a new model of learning.

A MECHANISTIC VIEW

At the moment, we are suffering the consequences produced by a long-standing form of education that regards knowledge in a very specific and practical way. Many traditional venues for teaching—such as the classroom, the workplace, and even books and instructional videos—have been predicated on what we would describe as a *mechanistic* approach: Learning is treated as a series of steps to be mastered, as if students were being taught how to operate a machine or even, in some cases, as if the students themselves were machines being programmed to accomplish tasks. The ultimate endpoint of a mechanistic perspective is efficiency: The goal is to learn as much as you can, as fast as you can. In this teaching-based approach, standardization is a reasonable way to do this, and testing is a reasonable way to measure the result. The processes that necessarily occur to reach the goal, therefore, are considered of little consequence in and of themselves. They are valued only for the results they provide.

LEARNING ENVIRONMENTS

We believe, however, that learning should be viewed in terms of an environment—combined with the rich resources provided by the digital information network—where the context in which learning happens, the boundaries that define it, and the students, teachers, and information within it all coexist and shape each other in a mutually reinforcing way. Here, boundaries serve not only as constraints but also, oftentimes, as catalysts for innovation. Encountering boundaries spurs the imagination to become more active in figuring out novel solutions within the constraints of the situation or context.

Environments with well-defined and carefully constructed boundaries are not usually thought of as standardized, nor are they tested and measured. Rather, they can be described as a set of pressures that nudge and guide change. They are substrates for evolution, and they move at varying rates of speed.

By reframing the discussion this way, we can see how the new culture of learning will augment—rather than replace—

traditional educational venues. For example, people today often describe schools as "broken." At first, it seems hard to argue with that. But what the proponents of that position mean is that schools have ceased to function efficiently; they are failing as machines. If we change the vocabulary and consider schools as learning environments, however, it makes no sense to talk about them being broken because environments don't break.

Rather, we look at the question in terms of how our schools' environments blend—or fail to blend—with the freedom and wealth of the digital information network. When viewed from this perspective, the learning that goes on in the school environment becomes more of an organic process, and the focus of the discussion changes from fixing a problem to growing a solution.

A SPECIAL TYPE OF CULTURE

Typically, when we think of a culture, we think of an existing, stable entity that changes and evolves over long periods of time. Individuals can choose to join cultures, but no individual can create one. What becomes important in this traditional sense of culture is the process through which people join a culture and the transformation that occurs as a result. We can imagine certain people joining a culture and changing it wholesale, but, for the most part, the process works the other way. When individuals become part of a new culture, they are generally the ones who are transformed. Consider an exchange student who has just arrived in a foreign country, for example. As he becomes immersed in the new culture, he undergoes a process of transformation in which he either adapts to the customs and conventions of the new culture and becomes integrated into it or finds he cannot adapt and elects to leave.

What we want to explore is a second sense of culture, one that inverts the process. In this second sense, a culture is what a scientist grows in a petri dish in a lab under controlled conditions, with very limited foreknowledge of what will result.[2] One of the basic principles of this kind of cultivation is that you don't interfere with the process, because it is the process itself that is interesting. In fact, the entire point of the experiment is to allow the culture to reproduce in an uninhibited, completely organic way, within the constraints of medium and environment—and then see what happens.

Unlike the traditional sense of culture, which strives for stability and adapts to changes in its environment only when forced, this emerging culture responds to its surroundings organically. It does not adapt. Rather, it *thrives* on change, integrating it into its process as one of its environmental variables and creating further change. In other words, it forms a symbiotic relationship with the environment. This is the type of culture that exists in the new culture of learning. It makes no sense to think of people adapting to what they are already doing. But it does make sense to see them as functioning within a broader culture and creating it, rather than merely responding to it.

THE NEW CULTURE OF LEARNING

From this perspective, therefore, the primary difference between the teaching-based approach to education and the learning–based approach is that in the first case the culture *is* the environment, while in the second case, the culture *emerges* from the environment—and grows along with it. In the new culture of learning, the classroom as a model is replaced by learning environments in which digital media provide access to a rich source of information and play, and the processes that occur within those environments are integral to the results.

A second difference is that the teaching-based approach focuses on teaching us *about* the world, while the new culture of learning focuses on learning through engagement *within* the world.

Finally, in the teaching-based approach, students must prove that they have received the information transferred to them—that they quite literally "get it." As we will see, however, in the new culture of learning the point is to embrace what we don't know, come up with better questions about it, and continue asking those questions in order to learn more and more, both incrementally and exponentially. The goal is for each of us to take the world in and make it part of ourselves. In doing so, it turns out, we can re-create it.

3
EMBRACING CHANGE

Change has been a subject for philosophical meditation throughout human history. The Greek philosopher Heraclitus observed, "No man ever steps in the same river twice, for it's not the same river and he's not the same man." What he meant was that by the time you remove your foot from the water and put it back in again, both the river and the person have changed.

Throughout the twentieth century, particularly after the Second World War, we had a slow-moving river. Stability, continuity, and maintaining the status quo defined our culture, and progress was carefully controlled. This environment influenced both education and technology.

EDUCATION

In the traditional view of teaching, information is transferred from one person (the teacher) to another (the student).

It presumes the existence of knowledge that both is worth communicating and doesn't tend to change very much over time. Ironically, however, it is that very stability that makes the model impossible to maintain as the world roils in a state of constant flux.

Many educators, for example, consider the principle underlying the adage, "Give a man a fish and feed him for a day, teach a man to fish and feed him for a lifetime," to represent the height of educational practice today. Yet it is hardly cutting edge. It assumes that there will always be an endless supply of fish to catch and that the techniques for catching them will last a lifetime.

And therein lies the major pitfall of the twenty-first century's teaching model—namely, the belief that most of what we know will remain relatively unchanged for a long enough period of time to be worth the effort of transferring it. Certainly there are some ideas, facts, and concepts for which this holds true. But our contention is that the pool of unchanging resources is shrinking, and that the pond is providing us with fewer and fewer things that we can even identify as fish anymore.

TECHNOLOGY

Advances in technology during the middle of the past century reflect just how gradually change used to occur. The development of color television is a particularly good example.

Bell Labs developed the first color signal in 1929, and RCA demonstrated it for the first time in 1940. During the following year, two of the three major broadcast networks (NBC and CBS; ABC did not participate) began field tests for color television. In the early 1950s, networks experimented with color broadcasting, and color signals went through a three-year period of standardization to meet FCC broadcast regulations. Prime-time shows in color were first aired by all three networks in 1966, and in 1972 the number of color televisions in American households finally surpassed the number of black-and-white sets. By 1999, according to Neilson, 68% of U.S. households had a television.[3]

Now compare those numbers to the figures for adopting Internet technology: In 1997, 18% of families had Internet access in their homes. By 2001, that number had grown to 50%. Two years later, it was up to 55%. By 2006, it had risen to 65%.[4] In 2008, it was 73%.[5]

Thus, it took 70 years to go from the first color signal to widespread adoption of color television. And the adoption itself could not have been easier: All you had to do was buy a TV.

Going online is a different story. Over a ten-year period, for example, most users will have owned several different computers, installed or learned multiple operating systems, and gone through dozens of e-mail clients, web browsers, news readers, and video players. Their software will have been altered, updated, patched, and revised numerous times. They will have discovered and migrated to and from hundreds of websites and may have created a host of identities, e-mail addresses, and points of contact. If you ask anyone who has been on the Internet for at least a decade what has changed, the answer will probably be, "Everything."

And the changes are not just skin deep. The infrastructure will expand to accommodate them—it may, in fact, be driving them. In terms of bandwidth alone, YouTube's website in 2007 took up more bandwidth than did the entire Internet in the year 2000.[6] What's more, YouTube would have been a failure back then: Broadband (which is required to stream video), fast processors, and high-end video cards did not yet exist, and the ability to create, digitize, and distribute digital content had not yet been developed.

Today, broadband is everywhere, digital cameras and webcams are either already built into machines or available very inexpensively, and all new computers can stream digital content. Indeed, many cell phones now have more computing power and Internet access than the average home computer did in 2000. The advances in processors, power consumption, bandwidth, and storage have all increased at a remarkable rate, doubling roughly every 18 months. The things that are commonplace in 2010 were unthinkable just ten years ago. As information is constantly produced, consumed, updated, and altered, new practices of reading, writing, thinking, and learning have evolved with it.

The Internet, in particular, has changed the way we think of both technology and information. Technology is no longer just a fast way of transporting information from one place to another, and the information it moves is no longer static. Instead, information technology has become a participatory medium, giving rise to an environment that is constantly being changed and reshaped by the participation itself. The process is almost quantum in nature: The more we interact with these informational spaces, the more the environment changes, and the very act of finding information reshapes not only the context that gives that information meaning but also the meaning itself. Consider what happens to a news story on a website that aggregates information from multiple sources. Just reading the story literally changes the shape of the news that day. As more people show interest in it, the story is moved higher up on the page and displayed more prominently. As even more people then become exposed to it, it gains yet greater prominence, and the significance of its impact continues to grow.

When change comes slowly, adaptation is easy. Many of the daily routines and practices during the past century involved managing change on a gradual basis. For instance, when a new technology came along in the workplace once every ten or 20 years, businesses could offer classes, retrain employees, hold seminars, or schedule retreats to bring everyone up to speed. In short, they could create structured, centralized learning tools to help people adapt. With shorter time frames, this has become more difficult: Retraining every year, for example, is burdensome (and is apt to create an alienated workforce). What happens, then, when you are dealing with change on a weekly, daily, or even hourly basis?

LEARNING TO EMBRACE CHANGE

Change motivates and challenges. It makes clear when things are obsolete or have outlived their usefulness. But most of all, change forces us to learn differently. If the twentieth century was about creating a sense of stability to buttress against change and then trying to adapt to it, then the twenty-first century is about *embracing* change, not fighting it. Embracing change means looking forward to what will come next. It means viewing the future as a set of new possibilities, rather than something that forces us to adjust. It means making the most of living in a world of motion. We can no longer count on being taught or trained to handle each new change in our tools, the media, or the ways we communicate on a case-by-case basis.

Many approaches to learning in the twentieth century did, in fact, work but largely because of the glacial rate of change that characterized the era. Memorization, one of the basic staples of education, is not a bad way to learn about things that seldom change, such as spelling, the periodic table of the elements, and dates in history. Unfortunately, however, what students memorize are things they don't actually use very often in their day-to-day lives.

Now consider the type of learning that has swept up an entire generation of children through J.K. Rowling's *Harry Potter* books. Ask any young fan about one of the main characters or about the significance of the scar on Harry's forehead, and the child will probably be able not only to answer your question but also to do so in great detail. Though it's very unlikely that she memorized the information, she learned it nevertheless. She absorbed it, like a sponge.

In fact, the kids reading the thousands of pages of text (the *Harry Potter* books, websites, wikis, blogs, and fan fiction) learned a lot about history, geography, philosophy, interpersonal communication, and basic sociology—and all without memorization. They did so by becoming part of the evolving story, which was told through seven books over the course of ten years. Each book in the series changed the narrative and managed to leave open questions about the fate, character, and role of many of the main characters right up until the end. The many possible permutations for the outcomes therefore spurred fans to create web pages, wikis, and thousands of their own stories set in Harry Potter's fictional universe. They organized meetings and conventions and formed discussion and reading groups. They even created a new genre of music, dubbed "wizard rock," that mimics the style of music referenced in the books.

To most people, that doesn't sound very much like "real" learning. What good are made-up facts absorbed from a fictional universe? Those people are missing the point. The important thing about the *Harry Potter* phenomenon is not so much *what* the kids were learning, but *how* they were learning. Though there was no teacher in this setting, readers engaged in deep, sustained learning from one another through their discussions and other interactions.

Kids learned the *story* of Harry Potter by reading the books. They learned the *meaning* of *Harry Potter* by engaging with the material on a much deeper level. Just as important, they followed their passion. Much of the pleasure of the *Harry Potter* series for this generation was about experiencing the unfolding of the story with friends, both online and offline. They anticipated, were energized by, and, ultimately, looked forward to the changes that each new installment brought to the narrative. In other words, with each new book, they were learning to embrace change.

MAKING CHANGE VISIBLE

Wikipedia may be one of the best examples of a system that embraces change. It may also be one of the best examples of the new culture of learning. One can look at Wikipedia from a perspective of either stability or embracing change and get two completely different readings of the site. In fact, the perspective you choose determines not only how you think about the uses of the site, but also what aspects of it you focus on.

In 2005, *Nature* published the results of a study conducted by Jim Giles, in which he compared Wikipedia's accuracy with that of its print counterpart, *Encyclopedia Britannica*. The study, which focused on factual errors, omissions, and misleading statements, found that Wikipedia and *Encyclopedia Britannica* were more or less equally accurate. News headlines announcing the findings generally echoed the sentiment offered in the title of Daniel Terdiman's CNET article: "Study: Wikipedia as accurate as Britannica."

The study, however, approached the comparison from the wrong perspective. What it really assessed was which of the two sources was more stable. If the study had viewed the question as one of embracing change, the conclusion would have been just the opposite: that Wikipedia and *Encyclopedia Britannica* are more or less equally *erroneous*—neither one gets it right. *Nature's* analysis found that in 50 articles, *Britannica* had 123 factual errors, omissions, and misleading statements, while Wikipedia had 162 (the numbers were deemed close enough to call them comparable).[7] The problem is magnified when you consider information that is not just factually wrong but has become outdated. Making knowledge stable in a changing world is an unwinnable game. What happens when a nation's name changes or borders are moved? How does a print publication deal with areas of science that are not only contested but also subject to radical change—or even reversal—based on a single experiment or new observation?

What Wikipedia can do, unlike *Encyclopedia Britannica,* is offer a very detailed record of the controversies over certain pieces of knowledge. And it does so exceptionally well. A quick glance at any Wikipedia entry reveals not only what the current, ephemeral, status of a given piece of knowledge is; it also discloses the history of any discussions, resolutions, and subsequent alterations to the entry that have given rise to its current form.

The Wikipedia entry for Christopher Columbus, for example, has been changed and updated thousands of times over the past several years. Those changes are stored and can be traced through a series of debates over Columbus's role in the history of the Americas. The entry reflects, in myriad forms, the shifts in opinions about the cultural, social, and political aspects of colonization, exploration, and the writing of history. Wikipedia allows us to read across time.

Print resources, however, in their attempt to create a

permanent record of stable knowledge, are forced to make choices that include or exclude similar material for reasons of form, content, or even organization. And by doing so, they render that information invisible. Imagine if we were able to see every aspect of the process for an encyclopedia entry, including the publisher's choice for who would write it, what the original entry looked like, what other people thought of the original entry, the edits and editorial decisions that went into the publication process, and the feedback provided by experts and lay readers. We would have a very different picture of what that entry represents.

Wikipedia allows us to see all those things, understand the process, and participate in it. As such, it requires a new kind of reading practice, an ability to evaluate a contested piece of knowledge and decide for yourself how you want to interpret it. And because Wikipedia is a living, changing embodiment of knowledge, such a reading practice must embrace change.

LEARNING THROUGH PLAY AND IMAGINATION

Embracing change and seeing information as a resource can help us stop thinking of learning as an isolated process of information absorption and start thinking of it as a cultural and social process of engaging with the constantly changing world around us. Once again, the experience of children can show the way.

Children use play and imagination as the primary mechanisms for making sense of their new, rapidly evolving world. In other words, as children encounter new places, people, things, and ideas, they use play and imagination to cope with the massive influx of information they receive. Child developmental psychologist Jean Piaget found that information became "susceptible to play" once it was assimilated and repeated, and that play was the means by which most children learn to understand the world from their earliest stages of development.[8]

Historically, the pattern has been that as children grow up and become more proficient at making sense of the environment in which they live, their world seems to become more stable. Thus, as a child grows and becomes accustomed to the world, the perceived need for play diminishes.

Today, however, children and adults alike must continue to deal with an ever-changing, expanding world. A child playing with a new toy and an adult logging onto the Internet, for example, both wonder, "What do I do now? How do I handle this new situation, process this new information, and make sense of this new world?"

This alters the formula: In a world of near-constant flux, play becomes a strategy for embracing change, rather than a way for growing out of it.

As we have argued earlier, traditional approaches to learning are no longer capable of coping with a constantly changing world. They have yet to find a balance between the structure that educational institutions provide and the freedom afforded by the new media's almost unlimited resources, without losing a sense of purpose and direction. Some posit that one of the primary problems with education, for example, is that our schools suffer from excess structure, which has no room for new technologies like Facebook and Wikipedia. Others believe that the trouble lies with insufficient structure, which cannot fully harness the power of new media and technology. Supporting either position may offer short-term payoffs but will fail in the long term because neither one addresses the shifts that are happening in the world around them. In other words, simply unleashing students on the Internet doesn't solve the problem any more than lecturing and testing them more does.

Similar problems exist in the workplace. The need for innovation—the lifeblood of business—is widely recognized, and imagination and play are key ingredients for making it happen. Yet while people in other adult learning cultures, such as amateur hobbyists, are innovating like crazy, workplaces have become relatively moribund.

The challenge is to find a way to marry structure and freedom to create something altogether new.

4
LEARNING IN THE COLLECTIVE

The new culture of learning is based on three principles: (1) The old ways of learning are *unable to keep up* with our rapidly changing world. (2) New media forms are making *peer-to-peer* learning easier and more natural. (3) Peer-to-peer learning is amplified by emerging technologies that shape the *collective* nature of participation with those new media.

We demonstrated the first principle in Chapter 3. Let us move on to examine peer-to-peer learning and the idea of the collective.

PEER-TO-PEER LEARNING

In the new culture of learning, people learn through their interaction and participation with one another in fluid relationships that are the result of shared interests and opportunity. In this environment, the participants all stand on equal ground—no one is assigned to the traditional role of teacher or student. Instead, anyone who has particular knowledge of, or experience with, a given subject may take on the role of mentor at any time. Mentors provide a sense of structure to guide learning, which they may do by listening empathically and by reinforcing intrinsic motivation to help the student discover a voice, a calling, or a passion. Once a particular passion or interest is unleashed, constant interaction among group members, with their varying skills and talents, functions as a kind of peer amplifier, providing numerous outlets, resources, and aids to further an individual's learning.

Learning from others is neither new nor revolutionary; it has just been ignored by most of our educational institutions. The college experience is a perfect example. When students set foot on campus in their freshman year, they begin a learning experience that is governed only in part by their classroom interactions. Assuming they live on campus, sleep eight hours a night, and attend classes three hours a day, students are immersed in a learning environment for an additional thirteen hours a day. Simply by being among the people around them—in study groups, for instance—students are learning from their environment, participating in an experience rich in resources of deep encounters.[9]

THE EMERGENCE OF THE COLLECTIVE

Our ability to produce, consume, and distribute knowledge in an unlimited, unfiltered, and immediate way is the primary reason for the changes we see today. One no longer needs to own a television station, a printing press, or a broadcast transmitter to disseminate information, for example. With just a computer and access to the Internet, one can view or consume an almost unimaginably diverse array of information and points of view.

But equally important is the ability to add one's own knowledge to the general mix. That contribution may be large, such as a new website, or it may be a series of smaller offerings, such as comments on a blog or a forum post. It may even be something as trivial as simply visiting a website. But in each case, the participation has an effect, both in terms of what the individual is able to draw from it and how it shapes and augments the stream of information.

This core aspect of education in the new culture of learning presents a model for understanding learning in the face of rapid change. Teachers no longer need to scramble to provide the latest up-to-date information to students because the students themselves are taking an active role in helping to create and mold it, particularly in areas of social information.

We call this environment a *collective*. As the name implies, it is a collection of people, skills, and talent that produces a result greater than the sum of its parts.[10] For our purposes, collectives are not solely defined by shared intention, action, or purpose (though those elements may exist and often do). Rather, they are defined by an active engagement with the process of learning.

A collective is very different from an ordinary community. Where communities can be passive (though not all of them are by any means), collectives cannot. In communities, people learn in order to belong. In a collective, people belong in order to learn. Communities derive their strength from creating a sense of belonging, while collectives derive theirs from participation.

In the new culture of learning, collectives, as we define them, become the medium in which participation takes shape.

They are content-neutral platforms, waiting to be filled with interactions among participants. As such, they are well designed to facilitate peer-to-peer learning, their raison d'être. And once they can no longer do so, their demise is similarly well designed. Since there are no bricks-and-mortar investment costs associated with their creation, collectives can simply cease to exist.

Give a man a fish and feed him for a day. Teach a man to fish, and feed him as long as the fish supply holds out. But create a collective, and every man will learn how to feed himself for a lifetime.

LEARNING IN THE COLLECTIVE

In a collective, there is no sense of a core or center. People are free to move in and out of the group at various times for various reasons, and their participation may vary based on topic, interest, experience, or need. Therefore, collectives scale in an almost unlimited way. In fact, they improve with size and diversity, providing access to an increasing number of resources managed by a technological infrastructure. Participation in a collective does not necessarily require a standard notion of contribution, such as explicitly creating content, but instead may be something as basic as following and rating posts on a website.

Thanks to digital media, the range of available collectives—along with their shape, design, and composition—is almost limitless. They constitute, in effect, an ocean of learning, providing innumerable possibilities for how people fish. What's more, since virtual collectives are not bound by physical or geographic constraints, they are generally available to anyone who wishes to participate.

The power of a blog, for example, rests in part with the

author or authors who start it; in part with the readers who leave comments; in part with those who link to, cite, reference, or respond to it; and in part with the readers, who may do nothing more than have their presence recorded by a web server. None of those events alone is sufficient for understanding the phenomenon; it is the combination of the active and passive (such as comments, ratings, and links) forms of participation that make a blog or website successful.

Blogs are a medium for learning, but they do not teach. Rather, they generate the space for a collective to emerge. It is impossible to predict what that collective will look like, and once it forms, equally difficult to manage it in any traditional way. Unlike a classroom where a teacher controls the lecture, the organic communities that emerge through collectives produce meaningful learning because the inquiry that arises comes from the collective itself.

At this point one might be tempted to ask how we might harness the power of these peer-to-peer collectives to meet some learning objective. But that would be falling into the same old twentieth-century trap. Any effort to define or direct collectives would destroy the very thing that is unique and innovative about them.

5
THE PERSONAL
WITH THE
COLLECTIVE

One of the greatest concerns about digital media today is that it may be rendering our lives too transparent. Almost every new media application provides some way to share personal information with friends, coworkers, or an audience. Twitter, for example, encourages users to answer the question, "What are you doing?" in 140 characters or less and then post the information so that anyone, anywhere, who chooses to follow that person's account can see it. Even more comprehensive is the idea of "lifelogging," in which a person documents her entire life and makes the information available online.

Critics fear that as a result we are losing a valuable distinction in how we think of our lives and how we share things with others. This distinction has often been framed in terms of the public and the private. The structure, arguably, can be traced back to the roots of much of western thought: Plato, and later

Aristotle, viewed rhetoric as speech for the masses (the public) and regarded philosophy as a subject for personal (and often private) conversation. Over time, the terms have more frequently been placed in opposition to one another, as public *versus* private.

Digital media, especially in the context of new social networks, have exacerbated the division. Objections to young people using sites such as Facebook or MySpace are often founded on the concern that today's youth are unable to distinguish between information that is appropriate for the public domain and information that ought to remain private. Digital cameras and sites such as YouTube have made it increasingly easy for people to share their innermost thoughts and private activities in a very public—even global—forum.

But is public versus private really the best way to frame the distinction anymore? Perhaps the fact that the boundary between the two is becoming so permeable indicates a need for a new way to think about the differences between them. We suggest a framework that has elements of both but involves intertwining and remixing—rather than opposing—domains: the personal combined with the collective.

The personal is the basis for an individual's notions of who she is (identity) and what she can do (agency). It is not necessarily private, though it may be, and it does not exist in a vacuum. We shape and define the boundaries of our agency and identity within the collective.

The notion of "the public" is singular, and it implies a sense of both scale and anonymity. The notion of a collective is more narrow. Collectives are made up of people who generally share values and beliefs about the world and their place in it, who value participation over belonging, and who engage in a set of shared practices. Thus collectives are plural and multiple. They also both form and disappear regularly around different ideas, events, or moments. Collectives, unlike the larger notion of the public, are both contextual and situated, particularly with regard to engaging in specific actions.

Sharing something personal with a collective, therefore, is very different from taking something private and putting it into the public domain. Collectives are not simply new forms of public spaces. They are built and structured around participation and therefore carry a different sense of investment for those who engage in them. When, for example, a person sings a song onstage at a karaoke bar, he is doing it within a collective environment. It may appear to be a public act, but it is very different from performing in the middle of Central Park or belting out a tune on *American Idol* in front of millions of viewers. The difference is that in the karaoke bar participation is not only valued, it is the substance of the activity itself. The collective that forms as a result provides an opportunity to do certain things (agency) and a connection with other performers who are similarly situated (identity)—neither of which exists in the other two venues.

THE NEW COLLECTIVE

Throughout life, people engage in a process of continuous learning about things in which they have a personal investment. Learning that occurs outside of schools or the workplace—through hobbies, reading, the media, and so on—is almost always tied to their passions. Yet although they are constantly learning about the things that really interest them, those things are rarely acknowledged in educational environments.

Classrooms, for example, are predicated on the sense of

the public and the private. Teachers stand before the group (the public) to lecture or guide discussions. Students sit in isolation, privately writing down notes, taking examinations, or listening to lectures. The goal is to transmit information in a public way to the private minds of the students. That's why a student panics when she is called on in class, even if she knows the answer to the question. It's because she is being asked to expose in public what had been until that moment a very private activity.

But consider any online site that caters to an individual's personal interests. A website dedicated to gardening, for example, makes no demands on its users; there are no tests or lectures. There is no public influencing of private minds. Yet learning happens all the time. And because there is no targeted goal or learning objective, the site can be used and shaped in ways that meet the needs of the collective—in this case, a group of people with a shared interest in gardening. Identity and agency within that space are both fluid, but they are defined by how the personal meshes with the collective. And that meshing, when it occurs, is likely to transform both the individual and the collective he or she is interacting with.

Such a transformation embodies both play and imagination. The interactions that occur in and around the collective force each member to open up his or her personal feelings about a topic to the group in a playful way. Adding one's personal perspective to the mix, and allowing the personal to be addressed and transformed through interaction with others, puts identity in play. The collective is, in the most basic sense, a group constantly playing with and reimagining its own identity.

The transformation of identity is not unlike what Benedict Anderson described with his notion of "imagined communities," which he saw as the direct result of the growth of print capitalism in the nineteenth and twentieth centuries. Anderson envisioned a sense of self and community emerging from the consciousness created by print. We see collectives as the creations of play and imagination in an era of digital media. They are, in that sense, a product of a changing world that can no longer focus on a single, national sense of community. But collectives are also a nearly infinite set of resources that any individual can selectively tap into and participate in as part of his or her own identity.

Almost every difficult issue we face today is a collective, rather than a personal, problem. And approaching some of our biggest challenges—whether financial, environmental, or health-care related—in terms of the collective has led to the development of meaningful solutions. One nonprofit organization, for example, has flourished using just such an approach. Kiva is dedicated to microfinance—lending very small amounts of money to people in the world's poorest regions to effect economic and social change. Funding for small projects had previously not been possible, since small loans are typically too costly for banks and other traditional financial institutions to provide. Yet as of July 2010, Kiva had loaned $147 million to more than 370,000 recipients in 200 countries using the World Wide Web as a platform. The average size of each loan was roughly $200, and the repayment rate greater than 98%.[11]

Kiva is changing the lives of people all over the world by fusing the collective (450,000 loan officers) with the personal (the highly motivated entrepreneurs who want to put their ideas into action). The organization funds businesses, of course. But it also funds passion, opportunities, and imagination, and it provides agency for the recipients of the loans. What makes it all work is not a traditional community but the participatory nature of the collective.

With its microloans, Kiva is creating a kind of learning environment (recipients need to figure out how to establish their businesses, get results, and repay the loans) that offers unlimited agency within the boundaries of its space. That unlimited agency is the key to the organization's success. Because there is neither a learning objective nor a right or wrong way to do things—and thanks to the possibility of funding—recipients of Kiva loans are free to play and imagine their businesses in a space they had never been able to before. Judging by the extraordinary rate of loan repayment, this highly personal approach works.

SEEING IN THE DARK

Author Timothy Ferris documented one of the most interesting stories about emerging collectives in his book *Seeing in the Dark*. The work was an effort to chronicle what Ferris calls a "revolution now sweeping through amateur astronomy, where depths of the cosmos previously accessible only to professionals or to nobody at all have been brought within reach of observers motivated simply by their own curiosity."[12]

The story goes like this. On February 23, 1987, a graduate student named Ian Shelton noticed the bright light from a star that had exploded thousands of years ago at the edge of the Tarantula nebula. He reported the find and was credited as the person who discovered Supernova 1987A. The occasion turned out to be an opportunity to confirm one of the prevailing theories in astrophysics at the time—that neutrinos (subatomic particles) reach Earth two hours before the light from a supernova becomes visible. As Ferris puts it, "That was the theory, but nobody had yet made any such observation."[13]

Shelton's report came two hours after underground detectors had registered a burst of neutrinos typical of supernovas. That alone, however, wasn't enough to confirm the theory. What was required was proof that the light hadn't already been there for a while—and thus arrived sooner than expected—before Shelton observed it. Enter Albert Jones, a New Zealand amateur astronomer who had also been looking at the Tarantula nebula earlier that night but seen nothing. His observation became critical in confirming the theory. Because Jones had seen nothing earlier, astrophysicists could confirm that the neutrinos had arrived two hours before the light from the exploding star. Pictures developed later that night by a third astronomer in Australia confirmed the finding. Ferris remarks, "If one were to choose a date on which astronomy shifted from the old days of solitary professionals at their telescopes to a worldwide web of professionals and amateurs using a polyglot mix of instruments adding up to more than the sum of their parts, a good candidate would be the night of February 23–24, 1987."[14]

In this story we can find the true power and nature of the collective. The amateur astronomers that night were simply doing what they usually did, following their interest and passion. But then the personal observations of a few astronomers (out of thousands) were fused by the collective (the combination of both amateurs and pros) into a meaningful set of data to interpret an event.

Because amateur astronomers are experts in looking and are spread out around the world, they are able to perform the Herculean task of watching the sky 24 hours a day and collecting data on what they see. Professional astronomers, who need massive amounts of data to analyze, thus rely on amateurs to do some of the intensive fieldwork required for contemporary astronomy. In response, amateur astronomers have begun not only networking among themselves but also linking their telescopes to provide better information and more sophisticated data. The result is a system of reciprocity, where both sets of astronomers are invested and take an active role in learning from each other.

COLLECTIVES AND EDUCATION

When considering the personal and the collective in the context of education, similar principles apply. Take, for instance, one of the most difficult and dreaded classroom activities: the group project. Students struggle to complete the exercise and teachers struggle to grade it. Why? Because our models of how a classroom works have no way of understanding, measuring, or evaluating collectives. Even worse, they have no means of understanding how notions of the personal may engage students. As a result, group work is almost always evaluated by assigning individual grades to students based on their contribution. What goes unrecognized is the fact that when groups work well, the result is usually a product of more than the sum of individual achievements. Even if a teacher does acknowledge that phenomenon and assign one grade to the entire group, the impulse is still to reward individual achievement (or in some cases punish the lack of it).

Now surf the web and look at any social networking environment, video, or art site. They are all group projects. No one dreads them, and no one has any trouble evaluating them at all. Kids today can tell you what sites are hot, what sites are passé and how different sites operate as different kinds of collectives. That's because their evaluations are based on how their personal sense of identity and agency matches with the various collectives that constitute different spaces. Increasingly, the Internet is becoming a place where the personal can begin to meet the collective in a meaningful way.

THE BIRTH OF THE BLOG

In 1999, a small company in northern California called Pyra Labs created a new piece of software that allowed users to write down their thoughts online and organize them into a web page that could be indexed with other web pages doing roughly the same thing. The pages were called "weblogs" (later compressed into "blog"), and they radically reformatted how people started to express themselves on the web.

At the time, the web provided a forum for public presentation, and search engines provided an organizing principle for finding and sorting information. But from the very beginning, blogs have been all about personal expression. During the program's first year of operation, Pyra Labs' home page described the process of blogging as easy and highly personalized: "You make posts to your weblog," the home page stated, "by submitting a form on this web site, and the results immediately show up on *your* site, with *your* design." This was the first time that Internet users could create a space on the web without some knowledge of HTML coding. The basic version was free, and the site hosted your blog as well.

The purpose of Pyra Labs' program, eventually renamed Blogger, was also unique. Blogger was meant to help people with common interests connect with one another, start conversations through blogs, and create networked conversations. Posting personal thoughts to the web had been one thing, but this was something entirely new: instant thoughts whenever. Blogs let people say whatever they want whenever they want to say it. And collectives are a natural outgrowth of those networked conversations.

The success of a blog depends on two things, neither of which is in the author's control: reader comments and external links. Blogs that survive and thrive do so because they create a strong collective of users who build conversations around an author's posts. An active blog garners attention from other bloggers, who then become part of that conversation by linking to it and commenting on it in their own blogs. The more links that feed into the original blog, the more popular it becomes, generating even more user participation, and so on.

By 2001, Pyra Labs had started describing Blogger as an "instant communication power letting you post your thoughts to the web whenever the urge strikes." The phenomenon exploded when Google acquired Pyra Labs in 2003 and integrated blogs into its search algorithm, allowing even greater and more direct access to the conversations emerging in and around the "blogosphere." With that acquisition, blogs moved from an emerging subculture to the mainstream. The fact that blogs could survive the transition is remarkable, and it illustrates something fundamental about the connection between the personal and the collective.

At their best, blogs give an individual the chance to interact with and become part of a collective that both shapes and is shaped by his or her thoughts. Blogs, by their very nature, are tentative works in progress. They have the character of playfulness, which is core to the new culture of learning. They can be experimental in nature, used to test and refine ideas. But at their base, they serve as a means to kick-start a collective around conversations about ideas that spring from the personal.

WHY HE BLOGS

Andrew Sullivan, a senior editor for the *Atlantic,* began his blog "The Daily Dish" in 2000. He recognized early on the transformative power of this new medium both in terms of the personal and the collective. For Sullivan, blogging is more than just journaling; it is journal*ism*.

In a remarkable reflection on this new medium, "Why I Blog" (November, 2008), Sullivan discusses how it is that blogs are beginning to remake the landscape of journalism: "The blogger can get away with less and afford fewer pretensions of authority. He is—more than any writer of the past—a node among other nodes, connected but unfinished without the links and the comments and the track-backs that make the blogosphere, at its best, a conversation, rather than a production."[15]

This change in authorship and authority is not unique to blogs. A similar shift is occurring in most digital media. Where authority had been traditionally vested in large corporate outlets, such as television stations, radio stations, broadcast corporations, and newspapers, it is now being decentralized among the many nodes that Sullivan describes. Institutional backing is no longer a warrant for credibility.

It is not that we don't trust the *New York Times* or CNN anymore. Rather, we have come to understand that their resources, though considerable, are in fact quite limited when compared to those of the blogosphere, which are limitless. Information put out in the blogosphere is investigated, challenged, and debated. If a statement of fact is wrong, someone will highlight it—and probably correct it. Institutional branding or a high-profile name alone is not enough to instill a sense of credibility today.

What Sullivan is describing, then, is a structural transformation of how communication happens. In blogging, authorship is transformed in a way that recognizes the participation of others as fundamental to the process. A blogger is not writing to an audience; he is facilitating the construction of an interpretive community.

Blogging is also a personally transformative experience. Because a person's blog is subject to change and revision by others, the influence of the collective can powerfully and meaningfully shape the blogger's view of the world, just as the blogger, at the same time, can shape the collective.

Sullivan draws two parallels to music that illustrate the phenomenon. In the first, he writes, "There are times, in fact, when a blogger feels less like a writer than an online disc jockey, mixing samples of tunes and generating new melodies through mashups while also making his own music. He is both artist and producer—and the beat always goes on." With that observation, Sullivan captures a sense of the new form of interactivity that modern media invites, possessing an inherent malleability that is directed toward social ends.

In his second comparison between new media and music, Sullivan states, "To use an obvious analogy, jazz entered our civilization much later than composed, formal music. But it hasn't replaced it; and no jazz musician would ever claim that it could. Jazz merely demands a different way of playing and listening, just as blogging requires a different mode of writing and reading. Jazz and blogging are intimate, improvisational, and individual—but also inherently collective. And the audience talks over both."

Substitute "new culture of learning" for "jazz" and "traditional forms of education" for "composed, formal music," and we couldn't have said it better ourselves.

TAKING THE EASY WAY OUT

The combination of the personal and collective defines many of the successes of web 2.0. Social networking sites such as MySpace and Facebook allow people to create spaces on the web that are both personal (in the sense that they reflect an individual's taste, interests, and activities) and collective (in the sense that they give users a way to create connections with others who have similar interests). Often referred to as "friend-of-a-friend" networks, they create a collective sense of belonging based on those shared interests.

These emerging new media platforms bring to the table two groundbreaking elements. The first is that they provide a means for truly harnessing the collective. Through the new media, the collective serves not only as a kind of resource for learning but also as a kind of amplifier: It intensifies and heightens the process of learning by continuously relating it back to the personal. The second is that digital media is based on an infrastructure that is designed to scale.

Harnessing the collective. Because learning with digital media occupies a space that is both personal and collective, people can share experience as well as knowledge. Here, people are not just learning *from* one another, they are learning *with* one another. University study groups provide a classic example.

A line of research begun by Harvard University professor Richard J. Light demonstrated that study groups dramatically increase the success of college students in the classroom. Further studies have shown that virtual study groups also work and that more casual forms of virtual learning, supported by social media, can extend well beyond the campus and reach a much broader audience. Consider the following observation, for example: "Although about 40,000 students are enrolled in classes on the university's campus in Ann Arbor, Vice Provost King believes that the actual number of students being reached by the school today is closer to 250,000. For the past few years, he points out, incoming students have been bringing along their online social networks, allowing them to stay in touch with their old friends and former classmates through tools like SMS, IM, Facebook, and MySpace. Through these continuing connections, the University of Michigan students can extend the discussions, debates, bull sessions, and study groups that naturally arise on campus to include their broader networks. Even though these extended connections were not developed to serve educational purposes, they amplify the impact that the university is having while also benefiting students on campus."[16]

Not all universities, however, share that view. In 2008, Chris Avenir, then a freshman at Ryerson University, in Toronto, created a virtual study group on Facebook called "Dungeons/Mastering Chemistry Solutions," which was named after a Ryerson study room on campus known as "The Dungeon." A total of 146 students joined the group, which was designed to help students solve homework problems. Since face-to-face study groups at Ryerson were common, and the university had already addressed any potential for cheating by giving each student a unique and distinct problem to solve, Avenir felt that working in a virtual group was just like working in a traditional one. As he put it, "This isn't any different from any library study groups or peer tutoring that has been happening."

By organizing this group, Avenir took a highly personal problem and formed a collective to deal with it creatively. The university, however, didn't see it that way and charged Avenir with 147 counts of academic misconduct: one for organizing the group to begin with and the remainder for each additional member of the group. When faced with the emergence of a new collective, the faculty and administrators of Ryerson were unable to comprehend it as anything other than a combination of individuals.

The university cited three reasons for pursuing the case against Avenir. First, it argued that learning should be hard. According to James Norrie, the spokesperson for Ryerson, "We want them to achieve. But that also means that they sometimes have to do the hard work of learning and not take the easy way out." Second, the school pointed out that the lack of structure for control and regulation of online behavior made virtual study groups incompatible with academic work. "It is not fair to students," Norrie argued, "to perpetuate the myth—and it is a myth—that they can do what they like online and that they're protected because that's only a forum for young people where they can do what they want to do, and that's really not accurate." Finally, the university saw the emerging online tools as a threat. As Norrie described it: "It is our job to protect academic integrity from any threat. And if that threat comes from new online tools, we have a responsibility as academics to understand the risks, to assess those risks and threats, and to educate people about how to avoid misconduct."[17]

In essence, therefore, Ryerson's objections to the Facebook study group, which was nothing more than a digital re-creation of the physical-world study groups that have been around for centuries, were that it made learning easy, allowed students to do whatever they wanted, and *as a result* threatened academic integrity. In Ryerson's view, apparently, learning must be both difficult and directed by others to meet the standard for academic rigor.

In March 2008, a Ryerson faculty panel adjudicated Avenir's case, and he was cleared of all charges. In a seven-page ruling, the panel found "no proof the Facebook group led to cheating."[18] Students had instead been using the group as a collaborative problem-solving tool. As Avenir explained it, "So we each would be given chemistry questions and if we were having trouble, we'd post the question and say: 'Does anyone get how to do this one? I didn't get it right and I don't know what I'm doing wrong.' Exactly what we would say to each other if we were sitting in the Dungeon."

Scale. At first glance, the Ryerson study group may not seem to scale. One-hundred-forty-six members constitute a very large study group, certainly larger than would be manageable or efficient for face-to-face interactions. But the group does scale in terms of the ability to engage asynchronously with others and to persist over time. Both of those things eliminate the basic physical constraints of time and space and open up countless possibilities for interaction. Members can present personal problems to the collective in ways that surpass simple question-and-answer sessions. In short, even if a problem is not *your* particular problem, you can learn by watching how it is worked out.

The students in the Ryerson study group were not 146 individuals, each working on one problem; they were one collective working on 146 distinct problems. By working through all the different points at which others became stuck in their problems, each member of the collective encountered more theories and applications of chemistry than they had ever done in a classroom or traditional study group.

All the elements of Facebook—content, approaches, personal investments, depth of information, and so on—combined to make forming a study group in which the students could do "whatever they want" very easy. And they learned far more as a collective than they could possibly have done individually.

CONCERTED CULTIVATION

The learning that happens through blogs, social networks, and other new media may be deeply grounded in experience and personal expression, but it also arises from the contributions of multiple people and voices. Expertise and authority are dispersed rather than centralized, and once a digital space hits a point of critical mass, it is very likely that some member of the community will have valuable expertise to share about a given topic.

We borrow from Annette Lareau the concept of *concerted cultivation* and then extend it to describe how people learn by watching and experiencing the digital world around them. Concerted cultivation has been remarkably influential in the study of the sociology of education, beginning with Lareau's book *Unequal Childhoods: Class, Race, and Family Life*[19] and continuing with dozens of studies documenting the importance of the connection between socialization and education.

What Lareau found was that children who live in lower-income homes perform significantly less well in school as a direct result of poor educational attitudes and a lack of exposure to educational resources at home. Over the summer break, for example, students from higher-income homes made significant gains in reading skills while those from lower-income homes tended to fall behind. Lareau concluded that families from higher-income homes were more likely than lower-income families to provide the cultural and social resources to promote reading.

We believe that Lareau's fundamental insights hold true in a wide range of areas in the digital world. In nearly every aspect of digital culture, structures are emerging that provide concerted cultivation for both general attitudes toward learning and specific approaches to skills or areas of interest. Unlike in past decades, however, concerted cultivation in the twenty-first century will value peer-to-peer interaction and the fluid nature and impermanence of collectives.

We don't mean to suggest that every interaction with the new media creates a learning environment. Rather, we suggest that each collective has the potential to make learning fun and easy and to allow people to follow their desires and passions in productive and fruitful ways.

COLLECTIVES IN THE ARC OF LIFE

The connection between the personal and collective is a key ingredient in lifelong learning. Amateur astronomers looking to the sky for new discoveries, Andrew Sullivan blogging, college students studying, and kids reading over their summer break all demonstrate how pervasive this dynamic is in our contemporary landscape for learning. They also all point to the same thing: the fact that technology has now made connecting personal interests to collectives possible, easy, fun, and playful because people are inspired to think past the boundaries and limitations of their current situations. Kiva's funding of microloans, for example, does more than make new businesses in the developing world possible; it makes them *imaginable*.

As we have seen, collectives change and shift in relation to the world around them, and new technologies are making it easier to access them. As a result, collectives are beginning to emerge throughout the arc of life—from preschool to old age. Learning in an age of constant change simply never stops. In the new culture of learning, the bad news is that we rarely reach any final answers. But the good news is that we get to play again, and we may find even more satisfaction in continuing the search.

6
WE KNOW MORE THAN WE CAN SAY

Traditionally, a person who can answer a given question is said to "know" the answer. We say that person has *explicit* knowledge. It is content that is easily identified, articulated, transferred, and testable. But it's not the only kind of knowledge there is.

Michael Polanyi, a scientist turned philosopher, wrote a great deal about the concepts of knowledge and knowing. In a short book called *The Tacit Dimension,* he begins with a very simple premise: "We know more than we can tell." What he describes is the *tacit* dimension of knowledge, which is the component of knowing that is assumed, unsaid, and understood as a product of experience and interaction—like what the *Harry Potter* fans we discussed in Chapter 3 experienced.

Police sketch artists are among those who have learned how to exploit the tension between the explicit and the tacit. They never ask for a description of the whole face they need to draw;

instead, they want to know about specific features, such as the eyes, nose, cheeks, mouth, and chin. It turns out that while people are very good at describing those things, they're not very good at communicating how they all come together. Police sketch artists, therefore, record the bits of explicit information they've been given and then fill in the tacit dimension themselves.

Like scientists cultivating bacteria in a petri dish, police sketch artists bring together descriptions of enough features to organically grow the whole picture of the face within a carefully controlled and regulated environment. What they have mastered is not the ability to draw a particular face. Instead, they have learned a process of which cultivation is an integral part. Best of all is that the process works with any face, at any time, under any circumstances.

TACIT LEARNING

In the old culture of learning, educational institutions and practices focused almost exclusively on explicit knowledge, leaving the tacit dimension to build gradually on its own, over time. Why? Because they could. Knowledge was valued in the old culture because it was seen as stable. It was thought to transcend time and place. Conversely, knowledge that changed—"yesterday's news"— was good only for lining birdcages.

When information is stable, the explicit dimension becomes very important. The speed of light, for example, is probably not going to change. The fact that it travels at 186,282 miles per second has been well established and isn't subject to interpretation. Thus although the speed of light also has a tacit dimension, it is probably better taught through explicit communication, such as in a physics class. It is not the kind of information that is likely to be absorbed through personal experience.

For most of the twentieth century, the explicit was both abundant enough and important enough to sustain an entire system of educational practices and institutions that could be sped up and personalized to keep apace with any changes in content. The encyclopedia, which has its roots in the ancient Greek conception of rounded and complete knowledge, is a good example of the ongoing effort to preserve knowledge in a fixed form. In the 1950s and 1960s in the United States, companies such as World Book, Britannica, and Funk and Wagnall's marketed print encyclopedias to home markets. In the digital age, the encyclopedia tries to persist in the form of CD ROMS, such as Microsoft's *Encarta*.

The twenty-first century, however, belongs to the tacit. In the digital world, we learn by doing, watching, and experiencing. Generally, people don't take a class or read books or manuals to learn how to use a web browser or e-mail program. They just start doing it, learning by absorption and making tacit connections. And the more they do it, the more they learn. They make connections between and among things that seem familiar. They experiment with what they already know how to do and modify it to meet new challenges or contexts. In a world where things are constantly changing, focusing exclusively on the explicit dimension is no longer a viable model for education.

The problem is that almost every technique and practice we have for understanding how we learn has been about the explicit—the content—in a stable world. We have had no theories or mechanisms for addressing a world in which context is rapidly changing as well. Until now.

FROM TEACHING TO LEARNING

Much of what we understand about knowledge is filtered through the idea of education. Explicit knowledge, as we have seen, lends itself well to the process of teaching—that is, transferring knowledge from one person to another. You teach and I learn. But tacit knowledge, which grows through personal experience and experimentation, is not transferrable—you can't teach it to me, though I can still learn it. The reason for the difference is that learning tacit knowledge happens not only in the brain but also in the body, through all our senses. It is an experiential process as well as a cognitive one. It is not about being taught knowledge; it is about absorbing it.

When a parent first tells a child not to touch a flame because it is hot, the child will almost always put out her hand and get burned. Why? Because the parent has given the child only a portion of the information she needed to make the decision—the explicit, cognitive part. He has shared only the knowledge he knew how to articulate: "Fire is hot." But when a child gets burned, her body learns all kinds of things that cannot be conveyed by such a simple phrase: It hurts. It is unpleasant. What's more, she learns not only to avoid the match that burned her but also to avoid things that *look* like the match that burned her, and she starts to make all kinds of connections to other things. That turns out to be the most important point. From that one experience, a finger touching a flame, a person learns countless things.

Because our minds, bodies, and senses are always learning, we pick up vast amounts of tacit knowledge just by going about our everyday activities—unlike learning through formal education, which takes place during specified, focused, brief periods of time. Our understanding and knowledge, therefore, are shaped to a far greater degree by the tacit than they ever could be by the explicit, especially in a world of constant change.

College campuses illustrate the phenomenon clearly. Within the old culture of learning, the value of a college education could be said to consist of the sum total of the accumulated explicit knowledge one learned and the techniques of learning that one mastered. But in universities today, as in other educational institutions, learning is happening outside as well as inside the classroom—in late-night discussions among students, in study groups, during campus events, and in student organizations. When that tacit dimension is taken into consideration, the value of a university education grows to include the learning that happens when students are immersed in an environment that values learning itself. Being surrounded by academic culture becomes valuable not only because of the vast resources available to the students but also because of the opportunity for them to make connections among all those resources—connections that are grounded in experience and deeply personal.

Measuring one's level of tacit knowledge, however, is a challenge. Traditionally, every new model of learning has had to specify how much knowledge actually transfers from teacher to student—the more the better being the goal. But the transfer model simply doesn't work for tacit knowledge. A student cannot ask his teacher to "give me your experience" or "tell me what it feels like to solve a problem" or "show me how to innovate." We learn those things by watching, doing, experimenting, and simply absorbing knowledge from the things, events, and activities around us. The skilled student today learns how to watch the teacher very closely and thereby infer what questions will be on the test. She's figured out that reading the teacher can be just as useful as reading the text for getting a good grade, and maybe for much more.

INQUIRY

Conventional wisdom holds that different people learn in different ways. Something is missing from that idea, however, so we offer a corollary: Different people, when presented with exactly the same information in exactly the same way, will learn different things. Most models of education and learning have almost no tolerance for this kind of thing. As a result, teaching tends to focus on eliminating the source of the problem: the student's imagination.

Imagine a situation where two students are learning to play the piano. The lesson for the day is a Bach prelude. The first student attacks the piano forcefully, banging out each note correctly but with a violent intensity that is uncharacteristic for the style of the piece. The second student seems to view the written score as a loose framework; he varies the rhythm, modifies the melody, and follows his own internal muse. In today's classroom, the teacher will see two students "doing it wrong." In the new culture of learning, the teacher will see a budding rock star and a jazz musician.

The story of these students illustrates a fundamental principle of the new culture of learning: Students learn best when they are able to follow their passion and operate within the constraints of a bounded environment. Both of those elements matter. Without the boundary set by the assignment of playing the prelude, there would be no medium for growth. But without the passion, there would be nothing to grow in the medium. Yet the process of discovering one's passion can be complicated.

In the spring of 2010, one of us was confronted with perhaps the most damning indictment of the educational system that we could imagine. Doug was teaching an undergraduate honors seminar, and the goal of the course was for each student to create a proposal for his or her honors thesis. The course covered all the various methodologies, techniques for research and for conducting reviews of literature, and guidelines for creating annotated bibliographies. Yet for the students, the most difficult part of the class turned out to be the first assignment, something that Doug had thought would be the easiest: selecting their thesis topics.

Students showed up in Doug's office with no idea of what they wanted to write about. So, in response, he would ask them: "What is it that you care most deeply and passionately about? What is it that you will wake up every morning *wanting* to write about?" He was shocked when student after student answered in roughly the same way: "I don't know. No one has ever asked me that question before."

Despite twelve years of grade school and three years of college, those students had never before felt as though their passion, the thing they truly cared about, actually mattered. In fact, the thought was so alien to them that, in almost every case, they had already rejected potential topics precisely because they were too important to them. They had come to believe that things they felt passionate about should not be part of the (formal) learning process.

This kind of thinking pervades current education systems. Yet most teachers know that when students feel passion for a topic, they will seek out the tough problems, rather than the easy ones, and work harder to solve them. And best of all, they will have fun doing it.

QUESTIONS AND ANSWERS

The new culture of learning is not about unchecked access

to information and unbridled passion, however. Left to their own devices, there is no telling what students will do. If you give them a resource like the Internet and ask them to follow their passion, they will probably meander around finding bits and pieces of information that move them from topic to topic—and produce a very haphazard result.

Instead, the new culture of learning is about the kind of tension that develops when students with an interest or passion that they want to explore are faced with a set of constraints that allow them to act only within given boundaries.

At first blush, this might sound like a standard classroom, where the teacher sets certain learning objectives and then provides the students with the opportunity to meet them. The difference, however, is that the structures that are put in place— whether they be textbooks, lectures, or assignments—are all intended to help the student learn a specific piece of information. In other words, our educational system is built upon a structure that poses questions in order to find answers. (In some cases, such as math, demonstrating how one arrived at an answer may be an important part of the process, but only because it produced the correct solution.) Yet finding answers and memorizing facts do little to inspire students' passion to learn. If anything, they dull that desire and make learning a tiresome burden.

We propose reversing the order of things. What if, for example, questions were more important than answers? What if the key to learning were not the application of techniques but their invention? What if students were asking questions about things that really mattered to them?

With that shift in thinking, learning is transformed from a discrete, limited process—ask a question, find an answer—to a continuous one. Every answer serves as a starting point, not an end point. It invites us to ask more and better questions.

LEARNING AS INQUIRY

The recent effort to use games for learning is illuminating. The reasoning behind the idea goes something like this: Kids love games, and they spend much more time playing than they do studying. So if games can be made educational, kids will play them longer and learn more—and they may even enjoy learning, too, which would be a welcome and added benefit. Consider a student who loves basketball, for example. A physics teacher might be tempted to take advantage of that interest by writing a problem set concerning gravity, force, and acceleration within the context of the sport. She might want to ask, "At what angle and with what force must a person shoot a ball to make a basket 20 feet away?" In doing so, she might think she has engaged the passion and imagination of the basketball enthusiast. But in reality she has done little more than cloak a typical physics problem with a basketball theme.

Now, imagine asking the question a little differently: "What is the best way to shoot a basketball?"

If the student has a true interest in the game, he will have seen countless times that the best players all use jump shots to score points, and that those jump shots all share similar mechanics. Now the student may become curious: "Why is that? What do they have in common?" He may turn to physics for an answer, but that will tell him only part of the story. Knowing the physics of how a jump shot works doesn't explain why it is the best way to do it. So he continues to dig. Where he will go with this line of inquiry is anyone's guess—it could be history, math, anatomy, physiology, sports psychology, or something else entirely. The point is that no matter what direction he goes in or what he finds, more questions await. And the questions he asks are limited only by his imagination.

We call this style of learning *inquiry*. It creates a motivation to learn and provides a set of constraints that make the learning meaningful.

Inquiry is an extremely powerful technique for learning because it produces stockpiles of experiences. Things that result in dead ends for one particular question may wind up being unexpectedly useful later on—even, perhaps, for a completely different question. The process forces us to explore the various ways in which information that we already possess can open up new sets of questions. Asking questions is not an act of demonstrating whether knowledge has been transferred. It is, instead, an act of imagination.

Inquiry is the process by which we ask not "What is it that we know?" but "What are the things that we *don't* know and what questions can we ask about them?" The possibilities of that exercise are almost limitless, but they are bounded by two important considerations. The first is the structure of the institution itself. Whether it is the workplace, the classroom, an Internet message forum, or some other venue, the norms and rules of the space dictate the boundaries of what can and should be the subject of inquiry. But perhaps even more important is the nature of the tacit dimension of knowledge.

Tacit understanding plays a key role in shaping the process of inquiry. And because it embodies more than we can say, it relates most deeply to the associations and connections among various pieces of knowledge. We run into difficulties when we want to follow these kinds of associations at the explicit level precisely because they cannot be named or articulated. But we can, and often do, speak of them as gut feelings, intuition, or hunches.

"It just seemed like the right answer" is rarely a sufficient explanation for choosing one response over another on a test. But hunches and gut feelings are not only acceptable when formulating questions for inquiry, they are, in many ways, preferable. Saying "It seemed like an interesting question to me" or "We figured we would try it and see" makes perfect sense in this context. That's because the process of inquiry results in useful information regardless of the outcome. In fact, you can sometimes learn more from taking the wrong approach than you can from taking the right one. When you focus on continually asking better questions, you rely on the tacit and use your imagination to delve deeper and deeper into the process of inquiry.

INDWELLING

There is an additional layer to inquiry that provides an important nuance to what we have been discussing as the tacit. The concept is a certain familiarity that forms through the process of prolonged inquiry on particular topics or from repeated use of skills and techniques. Polanyi has referred to it as "indwelling."

Indwelling is a familiarity with ideas, practices, and processes that are so engrained they become second nature. Not unlike the notion of inquiry, indwelling is also an adaptive process, meaning that the practices that become second nature have flexibility; they are responsive to changes in the environment and situation. They become an embodied set of practices that are both constantly changing and evolving yet also central to the definition of inquiry.

The more we engage with the process of asking questions, the more we tend to engage with the tacit dimension of knowledge. Indwelling is the set of practices we use and develop to find and make connections among the tacit dimensions of things. It is the set of experiences from which we are able to develop our hunches and sense of intuition.

When we think about engaging the passion of the learner, we need to think about her sense of indwelling, because that is her greatest source of inspiration, but it is also the largest reservoir she has of tacit knowledge. The basketball player who knows how to shoot a jump shot has not only a greater motivation to learn about biomechanics because it might improve his game, but he also has a vast stockpile of tacit information that can help inform him of what might be good questions to ask about how to shoot a basketball effectively. It is not just that the basketball player cares more. He actually knows things and make connections on a tacit level because for him, these are places where indwelling happens.

Traditional notions of learning can do little, if anything, with either this passion or this tacit knowledge because they are precisely the things that cannot be made explicit through answers. They can, however, be explored at a very deep and sophisticated level by asking the right questions.

With just a small shift, from answering questions to asking them, inquiry emerges as a tool for harnessing not only the passion of students but also the stockpile of tacit knowledge that comes from a lifetime of experience doing the things that have become second nature to them.

DISPOSITIONS AND THE NEW CULTURE OF LEARNING

For the final piece of the puzzle, let's go back to our two

budding pianists: the rocker and the jazz musician. One way
to describe their differences might be to say that each displays
a different *disposition* toward music. Under the old model of
learning, there was some question about whether dispositions
could be taught or perhaps nurtured. They have been likened
to learning styles that could be more or less receptive to certain
pedagogical techniques.

We think of dispositions as something quite different.
In our view, dispositions are connected to indwelling more
than anything else. They indicate how a student will make
connections at the tacit level. They don't tell us *what* someone
is likely to learn, but they do suggest the kinds of questions she
might ask and how she might approach answering them—in
other words, *how* she is likely to learn. A disposition is not
something that someone is explicitly taught.

People who play massively multiplayer online games provide
a particularly powerful example of how dispositions work. Today's
MMOs are large, complex, constantly evolving social systems;
in fact, their perpetual newness is the main attraction. Rather
than look for a particular solution to a problem, gamers tend to
marshal all their available resources and experiment with them
to find multiple ways of accomplishing a task. What they learn in
the process has less to do with solving a particular problem than
it does with learning the nature of the tools they have at their
disposal. Within the larger gamer culture, solutions that are new,
sophisticated, or unique are almost always preferred over ones that
are routine or obvious.

Gamers learn through experimentation. They play with the
tools they have in the virtual world they inhabit, repeatedly making
minor adjustments and recording the results. They might approach

the game methodically, going through a series of incremental steps, or intuitively, letting their experience guide the choices they make, but in either case, they rely on the connections among the things they know at a tacit level to achieve their goals.

Each generation of games begets a new generation of participants who share a common disposition. The disposition is made up of five key character traits that players bring to game worlds and which those worlds, in turn, reinforce. Gamers tend to:

Keep an eye on the bottom line. Today's online games have embedded systems of measurement or assessment. Gamers like to be evaluated and compared with one another through various systems of points, rankings, titles, and other external measures. Their ultimate goal, however, goes beyond rewards: They want to improve. Game worlds are meritocracies—leaders and players are subject to the same kinds of assessment—and after-action reviews are meaningful only as ways of enhancing performance (whether individual or group).

Understand the power of diversity. Games are designed to require teamwork; it is impossible to accomplish many of the tasks as a solitary player. Diversity, therefore, is essential, and the strongest teams are a rich mix of diverse talents and abilities. The criterion for advancement is not "How good am I?" but rather "How much have I helped the group?" Entire categories of game characters (such as "healers") have little or no advantage in individual play, but they are indispensable members of every team.

Thrive on change. Nothing remains static in a game. As players advance, they transform the virtual world they inhabit. Gamers do not simply manage change; they create it, seek it out, and feed on it.

See learning as fun. For most gamers, the fun lies in

learning how to overcome obstacles. Play amounts to assembling and combining whatever tools and resources of the game will best help them learn. The reward is converting new knowledge into action and recognizing that current successes as well as failures are resources for solving future problems.

Live on the edge. Gamers often explore radical alternatives and innovative strategies for completing tasks, quests, and challenges. Even when common solutions are known, the gamer disposition demands a better way, a more original response to the problem. Players often reconstruct their characters in outrageous ways just to try something new. Part of the gamer disposition, then, is a desire to push the boundaries of the environment in order to discover some new insight or useful information that deepens one's understanding of the game.

A few generations ago, a student with a gamer disposition would have been considered eccentric and difficult to manage. Students with that disposition today, however, are becoming the norm.

COLLECTIVE INDWELLING

Dispositions alone don't tell us how to construct particular learning environments. They do, however, indicate the potential for diversity of learning styles within an existing educational environment. In most forms of schooling, therefore, dispositions are problematic. Each classroom must be able to adjust to multiple ways of answering a single question, and teachers must have a thorough understanding of a countless number of dispositions—an unreasonable expectation for even the most dedicated educator.

But by reversing the question and the answer, as inquiry does, something that started as a liability—the radical differences among students and their dispositions—becomes an advantage. When the idea is to ask questions, diversity is a good thing. Moreover, students are both willing and capable of learning from one another in deep and profound ways. They turn diversity into strength and build their own networked communities based on interest and shared passion and perspective. In essence, they create and participate in their own collective.

The new culture of learning nurtures collective indwelling. Until now, we have lacked the ability, resources, and connections to make this kind of learning scalable and powerful. With access to the nearly endless supply of collectives today, however, learning that is driven by passion and play is poised to significantly alter and extend our ability to think, innovate, and discover in ways that have not previously been possible. Most of all, it may allow us to ask questions that have never before been imaginable.

7
KNOWING, MAKING, AND PLAYING

The truism, "you live, you learn," lies at the heart of the new culture of learning. A lifelong ability to learn has given human beings all kinds of evolutionary advantages over other animals. It is our killer app.

Yet despite the fact that our educational institutions do not embody that credo, and the old culture of learning is no longer suited for a world of constant change, current efforts are geared toward trying to fix the system by refining and perfecting it. A leaky bucket, however, will not begin to hold water if all we do is change the size and shape of the hole. So rather than patch the bucket, we propose three different, yet overlapping, frames for redesigning it. They are *homo sapiens*, *homo faber*, and *homo ludens*—or humans who know, humans who make (things), and humans who play.

KNOWING

Like Plato in his dialogue *Gorgias,* we make a distinction between knowledge and belief. Knowledge concerns fact and can be either true or false, while belief is always open to interpretation. "It is 100 degrees outside," for example, is a statement of fact, but "It is too hot to play baseball" is a belief. The first can be proved either correct or incorrect, while the second is up for debate.

Both concepts are situated as a question of "what." What is true at the moment? (It is 100 degrees out.) What is the best course of action? (Not playing baseball in 100-degree heat.) A question of *what* is particularly useful in terms of education because it is easily testable. In the first case, a person either knows or doesn't know a particular fact. The SAT, GRE, and other multiple-choice tests are designed to make that kind of determination.

In the second case, short answers and essays are better choices for evaluation because they call for test takers to explain and justify their reasons for believing what they do. We then judge and grade them on how well they support their conclusions with facts. If a person offers a quotation in response to a test question, for example, that quotation can be assessed for accuracy. What did the quoted individual actually say?

Up to and through the better part of the twentieth century, regarding knowledge as a static, easily transmitted *what* made sense, and it was the primary principle we used to shape our understanding of learning and education. Experts, for example, are people who are fully versed in the *what* of any given topic. In short, we viewed ourselves primarily as *homo sapiens.* In the twenty-first century, however, knowledge is becoming less a question of "What is the information?" and more of a *"Where* is the information?" Moreover, in a culture of learning where the context in which information has meaning is subject to change, reconstruction, and appropriation, the concept of knowledge being a *where* takes on heightened import.

In 2006, a survey conducted by Roper Public Affairs for the National Geographic Society found that 63% of Americans ages 18 to 24 could not find Iraq on a map of the Middle East. Robert Pastor, a professor of international relations at American University, described the problem as "geographic illiteracy." Two years later, one of us replicated the survey with a smaller sample and a slight variation.

Doug recruited 18 undergraduate students, also between the ages of 18 and 24. But instead of providing a map, he sat them down in front of a computer and said, "Find Iraq." One hundred percent of the students were able to do so—and more. They asked, "Street view or aerial?" "Do you want to focus on any particular region or the whole country?" "Should I turn the satellite imaging on or do you want it in map form?"

Clearly those students were able to complete the task with remarkable sophistication and detail. And the fact that they could call on multiple views of the map shows that they regarded it as more than just a marker of geography. They were able to use Google maps' interface to explore the richness of the technology to shape and reshape meaning. As a result, the map moved from being a moribund representation of geography to a new source of highly textured information, full of possibilities. In those students' world, facts have become things that can be located easily and at a moment's notice. Being able to find Iraq on a map was not a *what* question to them, it was a *where* question, which could be answered quickly and in very detailed ways. What this highlights is not the fact that the students did not attach significance to the *what* dimension of finding Iraq on a map, but rather that they attached a huge amount of importance to the *where* dimension. What their multiplicity of responses illustrates is that "Iraq on a map" does not just mean one thing, it means a multitude of things. And determining which of those things is the right one is more a question of where it means something than what it means in isolation.

Reframing knowledge as a *where* question underscores the increasing importance of context. In a world where context is always shifting and being rearranged, the stability of the *what* dimension of knowledge also comes into question. Only by understanding the *where* of a piece of information can we understand its meaning. This perspective also reshapes the notion of expertise. In the new information economy, expertise is less about having a stockpile of information or facts at one's disposal and increasingly about knowing how to find and evaluate information on a given topic. Again, this is a *where* question, both in terms of where the information is found and in terms of where it is being deployed to communicate something. It may be as simple, for example, as a magazine's name or placement in a bookstore, or as complicated as the process of evaluating authorship, sources, and origins.

The *where* has always been present. In fact, it guides almost all our daily practices. For example, someone getting dressed in the morning might pick up a newspaper, turn on the TV, or check the web to get the latest weather forecast; and mobile applications provide increasingly sophisticated forms of location-based information using GPS and databases. Today, friends are just as likely to recommend websites or applications for information about places or events as they are to offer the information themselves.

The shift to *where* alone is significant, but perhaps more vital is the fact that it also opens up the other two dimensions that emerge as cornerstones of the new culture of learning.

MAKING

Most traditional approaches overlook learning through hands-on activities, although it requires a deep and practical knowledge of the thing one is trying to create, and it can alter one's personal investment in learning considerably. For example, building a catapult, which may be a fun experiment for a group of high school students, entails putting principles of engineering and physics into practice. Accordingly, learning by doing can provide a unique and personal set of insights into the ways and means for creating something in the world. But something more radical lurks below the surface as well.

When we build, we do more than create content. Thanks to new technologies, we also create context by building within a particular environment, often providing links or creating connections and juxtapositions to give meaning to the content. Learning now, therefore, goes far beyond a simple transfer of information and becomes inextricably bound with the context that is being created. Where one chooses to post, where one links to, or where one is linked from does not just serve as a locus for finding content. It becomes part of the content itself.

Yet that is only part of the story. Through the process of making, we are also learning how to craft context so that it carries more of the message, which helps solve many of the issues of information overload. Thus, as context begins to play an increasingly important role, it becomes easier to talk about things like visual arguments; expanding the notion of literacy to include images, color, and sound; and how information is transmitted through new phenomena, such as viral distribution.

Take, for example, a film from the 1950s. If one were going to study and analyze the film, one would do well to know a little bit about the conventions of the period in which it was produced, such as world events of the time, prevailing cultural norms and values, and even the actors' level of fame. All those things offer perspective on the content and give it a richer meaning. In that sense, context informs content.

That context, however, is assumed to be stable and fixed. Today, new media tools let users restructure context in a way that allows content to remain stable but with a change of meaning. Think, for example, of a remix that does not affect a movie's visuals but alters the soundtrack to obtain a different effect, such as putting music from *Keystone Kops* in a chase scene from *Jurassic Park*. Through technology, imagination, and play, any given movie today can be changed into almost any other genre—drama, comedy, thriller, and so on. Meaning, therefore, now arises not from interpretation (*what* something means) but from contextualization (*where* something has meaning).

With those new media tools, then, we can take a static image—Humphrey Bogart from *Casablanca,* say—and reuse and reimagine it in countless ways, from serious commentary, to comedy, to political satire, even to advertisements. This is happening more and more. In an effort to parody John McCain in the 2008 election, for instance, comedian Stephen Colbert posted footage of the candidate in front of a green screen and invited viewers to reappropriate McCain's image for comedic effect. The challenge generated hundreds of submissions and YouTube videos. Viewers remixed McCain's image and words by using the green screen to change the context and place him in ridiculous or inappropriate settings.

This is not just about the production of new meanings and contexts that reshape old content, however. *Homo faber* also tells us something about the way we learn. Learning content through making is a very different exercise from learning through shaping context. In the first case, we are still concerned with the *what*, while in the second, we are concerned with the *where*. Both elements, nevertheless, are critical for understanding how one cultivates the imagination, and they provide the basis for what we think of as play. The process of making and remaking context is, in itself, an act of imaginative play (what we might call the "how" of information). Understanding that process and being able to participate in it also forms the basis for evaluation and judgment in the twenty-first century. By participating in the making of meaning, we also learn how to judge and evaluate it, giving special sensitivity to the ways information can be shaped, positively as well as negatively.

In a world where images, text, and meaning can be manipulated for nearly any purpose, an awareness of the play of context and the ability to reshape it become incredibly important parts of decision making. Since many of the places we now look for information do not carry the institutional warrants that have traditionally been used as markers for accuracy or truth, learning to navigate through and evaluate them—an expanded notion of literacy—is now critically important. We need to learn to read in a whole new way.

PLAYING

In his book *Homo Ludens,* Johan Huizinga argues that play

is not merely central to the human experience, it is part of all that is meaningful in human culture. Culture, he says, does not create play; play creates culture. In almost every example of what he describes as "the sacred," play is the defining feature of our most valued cultural rites and rituals. As such, for Huizinga, play is not something we do; it is who we are.

The concept of play is both complex and complicated. Nevertheless, play has been most often regarded as antithetical to the most stable pillars of learning in the twentieth century. It is the opposite of work. It is fun, rather than serious. And its connection to learning is secondary or incidental.

Play, we believe, in keeping with Huizinga, is probably the most overlooked aspect in understanding how learning functions in culture. It is easy to identify spaces in which the information network provides opportunities for play, online games being a clear example. But thinking about play as a disposition, rather than as merely engaging with a game, reveals something more fundamental at work. Much of what makes play powerful as a tool for learning is our ability to engage in experimentation. All systems of play are, at base, learning systems. They are ways of engaging in complicated negotiations of meaning, interaction, and competition, not only for entertainment, but also for creating meaning. Most critically, play reveals a structure of learning that is radically different from the one that most schools or other formal learning environments provide, and which is well suited to the notions of a world in constant flux.

Riddles and epiphanies. Through play, the process of learning is no longer smooth and progressive. Instead, there is a gap between the knowledge one is given and the desired end result. The gap is apt to widen in a state of constant flux, where stable paths and linear progression are no longer viable, thus making play particularly valuable in our ever-changing world. In Huizinga's view, this follows the structure of a riddle. Games researcher Espen Aarseth describes the dynamic as one of aporia and epiphany. In both cases, whatever information one has is insufficient to reach a conclusion about meaning or knowledge. Play provides the opportunity to leap, experiment, fail, and continue to play with different outcomes—in other words to riddle one's way through a mystery. That leap is more than simply a means to cross the chasm between what you know and what you want to achieve. It is, as both Aarseth and Huizinga propose, an organizing principle.

For Huizinga, the solution to a riddle does more than just solve it. It organizes and makes sense of the riddle. In that regard, our understanding comes not through a linear progression, in which each step confirms that you are on the right path. Rather, it arises through approaching the problem from many angles and ultimately seeing its logic only at the end. Riddles make sense only retroactively.

Similarly, for Aarseth, an epiphany does more than provide an answer. It throws all that has come before it into sharp relief by making sense of a progression that may have seemed disorganized, disheveled, or even nonsensical up until then. That is the nature of an epiphany. Reaching that greater understanding and finding the meaning could not happen without the playfulness of mind.

Agency. Unlike traditional notions of learning, which position the learner as a passive agent of reception, the aporia/epiphany structure of play makes the player's agency central to the learning process. How one arrives at the epiphany is always a matter of the tacit. The ability to organize, connect, and make sense of things is a skill characteristic of a deep engagement with the tacit and the process of indwelling.

What we do in play may best express the sense of becoming. Whatever one accomplishes through play, the activity is never about achieving a particular goal, even if a game has a defined endpoint or end state. It is always about finding the next challenge or becoming more fully immersed in the state of play. In play, therefore, learning is not driven by a logical calculus but by a more lateral, imaginative way of thinking and feeling instead.

The three dimensions of learning—knowing, making, and playing—are already beginning to emerge within the fabric of the digital world itself: Just look at what kids do today on social network and social media sites. Following a discussion of Mizuko Ito's work in Chapter 8, we trace out in Chapter 9 some of the practical implications of what a knowing-making-playing culture looks like in order to distinguish it more clearly from traditional thinking about learning.

8
HANGING OUT, MESSING AROUND, AND GEEKING OUT

In order to provide a glimpse of how students are learning in new ways, we include here an overview of Mizuko Ito's ethnographic studies of social media participation by youths and young adults. In this three-year, large-scale, collaborative project funded by the John D. and Catherine T. MacArthur Foundation, Ito and her team constructed a typology of practices to describe the way young people participate with new media: *hanging out, messing around,* and *geeking out.*[20] We believe that these three practices could frame a progression of learning that is endemic to digital networks. When we tie these notions of participation to the frames of reference we outlined in Chapter 7, we can begin to see not only how each level of participation produces a richer sense of learning but also how the affordances of digital media environments come into play in the construction of various learning communities.

HANGING OUT

At the most basic level, participation in digital environments requires a sense of "learning to be," which is more about acquiring certain social practices that give meaning to experiences than it is about any kind of abstract notion of knowledge as a thing or set of facts. It becomes a question of shaping one's own social identity. As Ito observes, "Through participation in social network sites such as MySpace, Facebook and Bebo (among others) as well as instant and text messaging, young people are constructing new social norms and forms of media literacy in networked public culture that reflect the enhanced role of media in their lives." Digital networked environments do not provide only an extension of real-world interaction; they also provide an enhanced environment for sharing information and engaging in meaningful social interaction.

Hanging out is much more than creating a feeling of presence or belonging. It is the first step in the process of indwelling, which, as Polanyi explained, goes beyond the process of enculturation and an understanding of social norms, roles, and mores. The beginnings of indwelling in the digital world are rooted in the notion of "being with." Ito's work reveals that hanging out is more than simply gaining familiarity with the tools, spaces, and possibilities that the digital world offers. Hanging out, in her terms, is about learning how to be with others in spaces that are mediated by digital technology. Thus, it is building a foundation for learning that transcends the bounds of the virtual. In essence, hanging out is a social, not merely technological, activity. It is about developing a social identity.

Thus the first aspect of indwelling, which hanging out begins to develop, is social experience. And social experience is governed by a central question: What is my relationship to others?

MESSING AROUND

The second notion of participation that Ito explores is messing around, which she describes accordingly: "When messing around, young people begin to take an interest in and focus on the workings and content of the technology and media themselves, tinkering, exploring, and extending their understanding." Within this framework, a second dimension emerges, one that not only engages playing but begins to bring the concepts of knowing and making into contact with one another.

The function of play in messing around, above all else, is to unpack and experiment with the familiar. We can see this in nearly every meaning of the word "play" itself, but perhaps most directly in relation to how we use things. Experimenting with the familiar in terms of content and tools is apt to open up a gap between this first unfocused form of play and the potential that emerges because of it. The gap is between the way something could be—what a person begins to imagine she can accomplish—and the way it is. For some users in digital environments, messing around, which is characterized by Ito as "open-ended," "self-taught," and "loosely goal directed" follows from hanging out. As people start to play in their environment, they rediscover the different possibilities opened up by those gaps. That rediscovery causes a shift in perspective, where the process of knowing stops being about one's relationship to others and becomes about one's relationship to the environment.

It also causes a shift in agency. Hanging out is about acquiring a sense of social agency. The transition to messing around, as Ito describes it, is typically personal and involves the development of a sense of personal agency: "...what is characteristic of these initial forays into messing around is that youth are pursuing topics of personal interest. Young people who were active digital media creators or deeply involved in other interest-driven groups generally described a moment when they took a personal interest in a topic and pursued it in a self-directed way."

We would describe that process as moving from experience to embodiment, where the personal investment in technology and digital media changes the focus from social agency to personal agency. When that happens, technology and digital media begin to be viewed as an extension of oneself. Not surprisingly, most of the introductions to messing around that Ito describes involve things that are heavily connected to personal identity, such as videos, pictures, profiles, and the modifications that players make to the games they play.

What messing around reveals most fundamentally is that the relationship between people and their environments is rich, complex, and changing. The process of knowing has moved from being instrumental to being structured by a sense of play. Through that shift, experience is transformed into a process of experimentation, play, and riddling, which reveals the resources and possibilities that are available to a person and what he can do with them. The flexibility he has in his own experience invites him to think through the possibilities of altering and experimenting with the things that are at hand.

Messing around, therefore, constitutes the second step of indwelling: embodiment. It asks the question: What am I able to explore?

GEEKING OUT

The final stage of participation, geeking out, is the most complicated. Within the frames we discussed above, there are two aspects of geeking out that merit particular attention. The first concerns the conditions under which geeking out occurs: the technological infrastructure that makes it possible. Ito describes it this way: "The ability to engage with media and technology in an intense, autonomous, and interest-driven way is a unique feature of today's media environment. The Internet can provide access to an immense amount of information related to their particular interests, and it can support various forms of 'geeking out'...."

Second is the manner in which geeking out extends both the social agency of hanging out and the personal agency of messing around. As Ito puts it: "Geeking out involves learning to navigate esoteric domains of knowledge and practice and participating in communities that traffic in these forms of expertise." For our purposes, this is the most critical aspect of geeking out.

The richness of experience and social agency produced by hanging out and the sense of embodiment and personal agency created by messing around, combined with the sense of making, produces what we think is the ultimate goal of indwelling: learning. Geeking out provides an experiential, embodied sense of learning within a rich social context of peer interaction, feedback, and knowledge construction enabled by a technological infrastructure that promotes "intense, autonomous, interest driven" learning.

This kind of learning highlights the importance of understanding the power of collaboration. It includes the ways in which the social functions of hanging out and the exploratory functions of messing around can be harnessed and compounded, through collaboration, to produce specialized knowledge networks and Internet-based communities and organizations. It emerges from a sense of indwelling, embodiment, and agency. And as a result, it gains almost all its power and benefits from the shared experiences that are part and parcel of collective indwelling. Collective indwelling is fundamental for the emergence of a networked imagination.

Geeking out asks the question: How can I utilize the available resources, both social and technological, for deep exploration?

9
THE NEW CULTURE OF LEARNING FOR A WORLD OF CONSTANT CHANGE

When we think about what a new educational environment might look like in the twenty-first century, we can imagine a number of things. Imagine an environment that is constantly changing. Imagine an environment where the participants are building, creating, and participating in a massive network of dozens of databases, hundreds of wikis and websites, and thousands of message forums, literally creating a large-scale knowledge economy. Imagine an environment where participants are constantly measuring and evaluating their own performances, even if that requires them to build new tools to do it. Imagine an environment where user interface dashboards are individually and personally constructed by users to help them make sense of the world and their own performance in it. Imagine an environment where evaluation is based on after-action reviews not to determine rewards but to continually enhance performance. Imagine an environment where learning happens on a continuous basis because the participants are internally motivated to find, share, and filter new information on a near-constant basis.

Finding an environment like that sounds difficult, but it isn't. It already exists, and in one of the most unlikely places: a new generation of games. Massively multiplayer online games—such as *World of Warcraft, EVE Online, Star Wars Galaxies,* and *Lord of the Rings Online,* to name a few—are large-scale social communities that provide a case study in how players absorb tacit knowledge, process it into a series of increasingly sophisticated questions, and engage collectives to make the experience more personally meaningful. What they teach us about learning is not specific to any game per se but is embedded in the collectives that are constructed in, around, and through the game. In essence, the game provides the impetus for collectives to take root.

Still, some educators continue to dismiss games as frivolous or time-wasting entertainment, while others ignore the distinctions among them and consider all games to be antisocial and violent, such as *Grand Theft Auto* or "first-person shooter" games. New research shows, however, that games can in fact aid and enhance learning. We go even further: In our view, MMOs are almost perfect illustrations of a new learning environment. On one hand, games like *World of Warcraft* produce massive information economies, composed of thousands of message forums, wikis, databases, player guilds, and communities. In that sense, they are paragons of an almost unlimited information network. On the other hand, they constitute a bounded environment within which players have near-absolute agency, enjoying virtually unlimited experimentation and exploration—more of a petri dish.

MMOs draw in players from every walk of life, of every

age, and across gender, class, and socioeconomic divides. They require an immense amount of learning in order to play them and are grounded in participation. Most important, the engine that drives learning in *World of Warcraft* is a blend of questioning, imagination, and—best of all—play.

UNDERSTANDING THE NEW CONTEXT

In *World of Warcraft,* one of the most successful multiplayer games ever, groups of players battle fictional monsters (not one another) in extremely complex group actions called *raids*. A group of 25 players, for example, will need six to eight hours, on average, to complete most raids. Raids require intense coordination, concentration, and participation from each and every member of the team.

To advance, players experiment within the game and draw from external information sources to construct a very sophisticated learning environment. They create standards and tools for measurement that rely on advanced mathematics, build statistical models and intricate programs for data processing, and conduct after-action reviews and teamwide performance evaluations. And they do it for fun in a social context.

Message forums such as "Elitist Jerks"[21] routinely post statistical analyses of game play, results of in-game experimentations, replications of previous tests, rankings of various techniques and timings of "spell castings" and attack sequences, and overall discussions of how to engage in what the forums refer to as "theory crafting." In theory crafting, players post programs, calculators, and spreadsheets to allow others to test and evaluate various combinations of gear and spells and report back their levels of success.

Guilds may constitute the most significant learning environment within the game. A serious guild might have a hundred or so players, and most guilds have some sort of leadership structure that includes positions of responsibility and offers various levels of membership. In almost all guilds, players are required both to participate—they can't just sit back and watch everyone else—and to advance the progression of the guild.

Raids provide the best sense of a collective learning environment. The goal of the guild is to proceed through a series of increasingly difficult raids, by which the guild's progress is measured. In each raid, the defeated monsters drop "loot" in the form of gear that will allow the guild to succeed in later, more-challenging raids.

The amount of learning that goes on in even the smallest guilds is amazing, as is the amount of data that gets processed, filtered, and integrated into play and game practices. The game's forums alone produce more than 15,000 new pieces of information each night. Yet guilds have found ways to avoid being overwhelmed by this mountain of data and instead manage it with surprising efficiency, using techniques that may be evocative for other institutions that face similar problems.

Guilds like the Garden Gnome Liberation Army (GLA), a collection of more than 100 players who twice-weekly engage in complex raids, sit at the intersection of the two elements that make up the new culture of learning. They are intensive and complex learning collectives that are deeply invested in constructing, utilizing, and managing large-scale knowledge economies (the information network). In order to succeed, every single member of the guild must take an active, constant, and enthusiastic role in learning information about the game, his or her character class, and the battles, fights, and challenges they will face. At the same time, the space of the world itself is fluid, changing, and dynamic. It presents players with boundaries within which they search for success through trial and error, finding idiosyncratic solutions to complicated problems. Solutions are not discovered so much as they are organically grown (as in a petri dish).

Gamers bring these two elements together through play. They combine the knowledge gained from outside the game with an evolving set of practices that occur inside the game, both of which feed each other. As players create new solutions within the game space, they return verbal characterizations, analyses, and videos to the knowledge economy surrounding the game, thus disseminating them to a wider group of players, who then use that information to create even newer solutions, and so on. In short, they in engage in inquiry. Within the new culture of learning, networked information provides nutrients for the petri dish, allowing exploration, play, and experimentation to continually cultivate new questions.

But perhaps the deepest level of play and, for our purposes, the most significant aspect of it, has to do with a sense of collective indwelling. When engaged in a game like *World of Warcraft,* one moves beyond a sense of just playing with others. In order to succeed, players immerse themselves in the game, creating and constructing identities, relationships, and practices that constitute deep and profound acts of imagination. And that act of immersion is itself, at base, an act of imagination and collaboration. Very few challenges in *World of Warcraft* can be solved alone, and none of them occur at advanced levels of the game. A guild's success depends on how well its members can synchronize their efforts to solve problems.

GLA members, for example, would spend months advancing through a particular raid with only incremental success each week. Eventually, the guild would have a breakthrough and suddenly be able to succeed at something that it had been failing to accomplish until then. At that point, a major shift had occurred, and in everyone's mind, the goal had become achievable. And shortly thereafter, usually, the raid would succeed, seemingly without effort.

So what changed? Not the gear the players possessed or their own skill levels and talents. Instead, there was a collective shift in imagination. As the fight unfolded one last time, the players—though dispersed all over the globe—had managed to completely synchronize their endeavors. Yet no one could articulate why they could do so on that day and not before. The knowledge acquired to defeat the boss and complete the challenge was principally tacit.

As we have seen, tacit learning functions most effectively when students discover their own learning objectives. Games, which allow learners to play, explore, and experience, also allow them to discover what is important to them, what it is they actually want to learn—and that keeps them playing. When people stop learning in a game, they lose interest and quit. When understood properly, therefore, games may in fact be one of the best models for learning and knowing in the twenty-first century. Why? Because if a game is good, you never play it the same way twice.

THE VIRTUAL SPACE OF COLLECTIVE INDWELLING

Raiding is an intricate exercise in coordinating and executing complex strategies. Each battle takes 30 to 45 minutes to complete (raids may have up to ten or 12 battles in total) and requires 25 guild members to operate in almost chronometric synchronization. Every player must perform up to his or her maximum potential, and in order to do so, each player's character must successfully fulfill the specific responsibilities of its class.

Perhaps most important, however, is that each stage is highly indeterminate; players only know what to expect in a very general sense. The monsters they face have a certain degree of artificial intelligence, meaning that they will respond to the context in different ways depending on a wide variety of factors. Because of the random nature of the monster's actions, therefore, a fight never plays out the same way twice. So while gamers may know the parameters of a fight, they never know *exactly* what will happen. Every player must be able to perform certain skills and be aware of movement, placement, and team organization at all times, and, to succeed, they need to operate seamlessly together, constantly adjusting and compensating for changes. If even a single player's character dies at this early stage, completing the fight becomes extremely difficult. The remaining stages all have the same kinds of uncertainty built into them, so players never experience any one of those fights in exactly the same way, either.

Members of a raiding guild have read plenty of information, gleaned from the information network, about what the fight would entail before they set foot into the dungeon. Yet there is no one "right" way to succeed. Each fight requires countless minor adjustments, which shape the events that follow it, making it impossible to predict what might come next. Knowing how the fight works, therefore, is necessary but insufficient for success. Information alone is just not enough.

Victory also requires a more organic notion of learning: experimentation. The three months of practice helped the GLA steadily improve, and as the members made progress—however minor—each week, they set new incremental goals to advance through the fight. Practice made the players more aware of their individual roles and responsibilities and helped them understand both the mechanics of the fight and the possible combination of things they were likely to see.

Yet neither the first notion of the culture of learning (finding information) nor the second (practice, play, experience, and creating new knowledge constantly) accounts for the leap from complete failure to easy success. Something clicked for the guild, something that had not been there before—a key positioning or transition between stages of a fight, a well-timed spell casting, or perhaps a new series of moves that tipped the balance and cleared the path to victory.

It's fascinating that no one in the guild could articulate exactly what had happened. In games like *World of Warcraft* this is a frequent occurrence. Oftentimes triumph seems to occur without reason; battles are won that, by all rights, should have been lost. Players find themselves wondering, "How on earth did we do that?" What's more, once that shift happens, players find that it can happen again, and eventually it even becomes commonplace.

We believe that this provides a critical key to understanding what we mean by a sense of collective indwelling—the feeling and belief that group members share a tacit understanding of one another, their environment, and the practices necessary to complete their task. Collective indwelling evolves out of the fusion of the information network and petri dish elements of learning, and it is almost entirely tacit. It both resides in and provokes the imagination. It is at once personal and collective. Though individual performance is vitally important—each and every player must execute the jobs flawlessly or the team doesn't succeed—it is inherently tied to the group itself. There is no way for a single player (or even a small handful of players) to succeed alone. The team relies on everyone to understand that their success as individuals creates something that amounts to more than the sum of its parts.

SHARED IMAGINATION

A game like *World of Warcraft* may seem to be a strange representative of an environment in the new culture of learning, but in many ways it is also the most appropriate. Throughout this book, we have constantly returned to the ideas of change and flux. And we have found that gamers embody the spirit of embracing change as much as, if not more than, anyone.

Games have grown up, and playing with them is no longer reserved for children. In fact, the ability to play may be the single most important skill to develop for the twenty-first century. In this context, play involves what we think of as a *questing* disposition. Questing is an activity that is central to most large-scale online games, and it presumes a number of things. Chief among them is that the world provides multiple resources and avenues for solving problems and that solutions are invented as much as they are implemented. The key to questing is not typical problem solving. It is innovation.

As we have seen, the things that are learned through MMOs are fed back into the collective through a variety of sources and gradually become adopted throughout their standard practices. What begins as experimentation is replicated, tested, and incorporated into the stockpile of information that constitutes the knowledge economy surrounding the game.

This type of innovation is also a fusion of the two elements of learning, a pulling together of resources and experimenting with them to see what fits. Through questing one finds what works and what doesn't for a particular problem, but either way one also gets a feel for each object or item one encounters. At the explicit level, solutions succeed or fail. But at the tacit level, players gain information about the item at hand regardless of success or failure. That tacit knowledge is a key component of indwelling. Without it, players cannot understand the collective or their place in it. Each one develops a personal relationship with the world that, in turn, becomes shared and modified as he or she interacts with others.

Once players start to interact, they also develop a shared sense of imagination that is the means for, and the object of, collective indwelling. The environment that is *World of Warcraft* is made up of the acts of shared imagination among its inhabitants. And what makes that world particularly interesting and challenging is both constant change and the fact that the actions of the players in the world, as a collective, are driving that change.

We look to gamers because they don't just embrace change, they demand it. Their world is in a state of constant flux, and it must continually be reinvented and reimagined through acts of collective imagination. That's what makes the game fun. But while players defeat bosses, kill monsters, coordinate raids, find new armor, and read blogs, wikis, and forums, learning happens, too.

WHAT REALLY COUNTS

From the perspective of learning, battling monsters and collecting treasure are the least interesting things going on in, and particularly around, *World of Warcraft*. Environments like *World of Warcraft* make it easy to see just how fun learning can be. They allow us to highlight the connections between knowing, making, and playing. They are places where we are permitted to let our imaginations run free.

That space of imagination is also scalable unlike anything we have seen previously. The information network and the bounded environment of experimentation (or petri dish) get better, richer, stronger, and more innovative with each additional player, new idea, set of data, and bit of information. The multiple collectives that make up the space in and around *World of Warcraft* process an astounding amount of information on a continual basis, seamlessly integrating new knowledge into play and action on a routine basis. Information flows and disseminates almost immediately. And as the game gets larger and more complicated, the new culture of learning works even better.

There are no answers in *World of Warcraft*. There is only a progression of increasingly complicated and more difficult questions. And, more often than not, those questions are the result of players pushing against the boundaries that the game provides. Players quickly discover that when they encounter a problem they don't know how to solve, the fastest and easiest way to learn the solution is to tap into a collective that is already working on it. Maybe members of the new collective will provide an existing piece of information that makes the problem solvable. Or maybe they will inspire a player to find a new, unique solution to the problem and share it with the collective in turn.

PLAYING TO LEARN

Think back to the assertions that Huizinga put forward in *Homo Ludens:* (1) Play is more than something we do, it is who we are, and (2) play precedes culture. We want to add to those concepts by proposing that play fuses the two elements of learning that we have been talking about: the information network and the petri dish (or bounded environment of experimentation). That fusion is what we call the new culture of learning. The critical idea is that the two elements—of information and experimentation—are being brought together in a way that transforms them both. It is that fusion that defines the new culture of learning.

In the first, play is the central tool for inverting the traditional hierarchy of learning and knowing. We believe that, instead of posing questions to find answers, it is essential to use answers to find increasingly better questions. When we address a problem like a puzzle or a game, we engage in acts of productive inquiry, where the answers we find become part of our stockpile of information, which can then be used to find better and more interesting questions as well as to solve future problems. And because these problems often take the form of a riddle that makes sense only in hindsight (when the answer is discovered), this productive inquiry requires—even demands—acts of imagination. Games and the worlds they happen in are helping us understand how to engage our imaginations both for play and for connecting to a collective. The second element—of experimentation, growth, and evolution—also emerges out of play. Both elements, when fused, accelerate dramatically once they begin to function within the collective.

By following Huizinga's lead, we can understand not only how each of these elements works individually and at a personal level, but also what happens when they come together. The result is a new form of culture in which knowledge is seen as fluid and evolving, the personal is both enhanced and refined in relation to the collective, and the ability to manage, negotiate, and participate in the world is governed by the play of imagination. As we watch the world move to a state of near-constant change and flux, we believe that connecting play and imagination may be the single most important step in unleashing the new culture of learning.

The almost unlimited resources provided by the information network serve as a set of nutrients, constantly selected and incorporated into the bounded environment of the petri dish, which provides the impetus for experimentation, play, and learning. Accordingly, the culture that emerges, the new culture of learning, is a culture of collective inquiry that harnesses the resources of the network and transforms them into nutrients within the petri dish environment, turning it into a space of play and experimentation.

That moment of fusion between unlimited resources and a bounded environment creates a space that does not simply allow for imagination, it *requires* it. Only when we care about experimentation, play, and questions more than efficiency, outcomes, and answers do we have a space that is truly open to the imagination.

And where imaginations play, learning happens.

NOTES

Chapter 1: Arc-of-Life Learning

1. According to the Institute of Play, "Gamestar Mechanic (G*M) is a digital
    learning platform developed by Gamelab and supported through a partnership
    with the Institute of Play, E-Line Ventures, and the Academic Advanced
    Distributed Learning Co-Lab (AADLC) at the University of Wisconsin-Madison.
    In Gamestar Mechanic, players learn the fundamentals of game design as they
    create games, and share them with a larger community of players. Within the
    game, players take the role of 'game mechanics' in a steampunk world where
    the rules and elements of games have come to life as creatures." See www.
    instituteofplay.com/node/162/.

Chapter 2: A Tale of Two Cultures

2. This is a foundational concept for what Ann Pendleton-Jullian defines as
    an "ecotone." "Culture, as the shared beliefs, customs, practices, and social
    behavior of a group *and* culture as the growth of biological material in a
    nutrient-rich medium, both rely on distribution as opposed to concentration of
    activity." See "Design Education and Innovation Ecotones," (2009), 26, http://
    bit.ly/l2azD.

Chapter 3: Embracing Change

3.   See "Television History—The First Seventy-Five Years," www.tvhistory.tv/facts-stats.htm.

4.   See Rebecca Lieb, "Most Americans Have PCs and Web Access," (October 28, 2005), www.clickz.com/3559991.

5.   See "IT Facts," www.itfacts.biz/73-of-americans-go-online-in-2008/11795.

6.   See Raul Goycoolea, "Last year YouTube customers used as much bandwidth as the net in 2000—how can operators keep up?" (July 10, 2008) http://blogs.oracle.com/raulgoy/2008/07/last_year_youtube_customers_us.html.

7.   See www.nature.com/press_releases/Britannica_response.pdf.

8.   Jean Piaget, *Play, Dreams and Imitation in Childhood* (New York: Norton, 1962), 89. More recently, Ellen Galinsky, in *Mind in the Making: The Seven Essential Life Skills Every Child Needs* (New York: Harperstudio, 2010) and Stuart Brown, in *Play: How It Shapes the Brain, Opens the Imagination and Invigorates the Soul* (New York: Avery, 2009), have made similar arguments both for the importance of play and the connection between play and imagination.

Chapter 4: Learning in the Collective

9.   This is not to overlook other elements of higher education, such as extension classes or community colleges, which provide substantial resources for nontraditional students and students who are outside the mainstream. Much of what we discuss later in this book applies equally well to these kinds of institutions in the broader learning ecology that we develop.

10. The concept has been used before in a number of different contexts, particularly around the notion of "collective action" in the work of researchers Margaret Gilbert and Todd Sandler.

Chapter 5: The Personal with the Collective

11. See www.kiva.org/about/facts.

12. Timothy Ferris, *Seeing in the Dark: How Amateur Astronomers Are Discovering the Wonders of the Universe* (New York: Simon & Schuster, 2003), xv.

13. Ibid., 283.

14. Ibid.

15. Andrew Sullivan, "Why I Blog," *The Atlantic Online,* November 2008.

16. John Seely Brown and Richard P. Adler, "Minds on Fire: Open Education, the Long Tail, and Learning 2.0," *Educause Review,* vol. 43, no. 1 (January/February 2008): 16–32.

17. See "Ryerson student fighting cheating charges for Facebook study group," www.cbc.ca/canada/toronto/story/2008/03/06/facebook-study.html.

18. See Mike Sachoff, "Student Won't Be Expelled Over Facebook Study Group," WebProNews (March 19, 2008), www.webpronews.com/topnews/2008/03/19/student-wont-be-expelled-over-facebook-study-group.

19. Annette Lareau, *Unequal Childhoods: Class, Race, and Family Life* (Berkeley and Los Angeles: University of California Press, 2005).

Chapter 8: Hanging Out, Messing Around, and Geeking Out

20. See Mizuko Ito and others, *Hanging Out, Messing Around, and Geeking Out: Kids Living and Learning with New Media* (Cambridge, MA: MIT Press, 2009).

Chapter 9: The New Culture of Learning for a World of Constant Change

21. See www.elitistjerks.com.

REFERENCES

Aarseth, E. J. 1997. *Cybertext: Perspectives on Ergodic Literature*. Baltimore, MD: Johns Hopkins University Press.

Anderson, C. 2006. *The Long Tail: Why the Future of Business Is Selling Less of More*. New York: Hyperion.

Bainbridge, W. S. 2007. The scientific research potential of virtual worlds. *Science* 317 (5837): 472–476.

Balsamo, A. 1994. Democratic technologies and the technology of democracy. *Cultural Studies* 8 (1): 133–138.

———. Forthcoming. *Designing Culture: The Technological Imagination at Work*. Durham, NC: Duke University Press.

Barab, S., and C. Dede. 2007. Games and immersive participatory simulations for science education: An emerging type of curricula. *Journal of Science Education and Technology* 16 (1): 1–3.

Barab, S., R. Kling, and J. H. Ray, eds. 2004. *Designing for Virtual Communities in the Service of Learning*. Learning in Doing: Social, Cognitive and Computational Perspectives. Cambridge: Cambridge University Press.

Barab, S., M. Thomas, T. Dodge, R. Carteaux, and H. Tuzun. 2005. Making learning fun: Quest Atlantis, a game without guns. *Educational Technology Research and Development* 53 (1): 86–107.

Barlow, A. 2007. *The Rise of the Blogosphere*. Westport, CT: Praeger.

Bartle, R. A. 2003. *Designing Virtual Worlds*. Boston: New Riders Games.

Bereiter, C. 2002. *Education and Mind in the Knowledge Age*. New York: Routledge.

Benkler, Y. 2006. *The Wealth of Networks: How Social Production Transforms Markets and Freedom*. New Haven, CT: Yale University Press.

Boellstorff, T. 2006. A ludicrous discipline? Ethnography and game studies. *Games and Culture* 1 (1): 29–35.

———. 2008. *Coming of Age in Second Life: An Anthropologist Explores the Virtually Human*. Princeton, NJ: Princeton University Press.

Bogost, I. 2005. Videogames and the future of education. *On the Horizon* 13 (2): 119–125.

———. 2006a. Comparative video game criticism. *Games and Culture* 1 (1): 41–46.

———. 2006b. *Unit Operations: An Approach to Videogame Criticism*. Cambridge, MA: MIT Press.

———. 2007. *Persuasive Games: The Expressive Power of Videogames*. Cambridge, MA: MIT Press.

boyd, d. 2008. None of this is real. In *Structures of Participation in Digital Culture*, ed. J. Karaganis. New York: Social Science Research Council.

———. 2009. Taken Out of Context: American Teen Sociality in Networked Publics. PhD diss., University of California, Berkeley.

boyd, d. m., and N. B. Ellison. 2008. Social network sites: Definition, history, and scholarship. *Journal of Computer-Mediated Communication*, 13 (1): 210–230.

Brown, J. S., and R. P. Adler. 2008. Minds on fire: Open education, the long tail, and learning 2.0. *Educause Review* 43 (1): 16–20, 22, 24, 26, 28, 30, 32.

Brown, J. S., A. Collins, and P. Duguid. 1989. Situated cognition and the culture of learning. *Educational Researcher* 18 (1): 32–42.

Brown, J. S., S. Denning, K. Groh, and L. Prusak. 2004. *Storytelling in Organizations: Why Storytelling Is Transforming 21st Century Organizations and Management.* Burlington, MA: Elsevier Butterworth-Heinemann.

Brown. J. S., and P. Duguid. 2000. *The Social Life of Information.* Boston: Harvard Business School Press.

———. 2001. Knowledge and organization: A social-practice perspective. *Organization Science* 12 (2): 198–213.

Burgelman, J. -C., D. Osimo, and M. Bogdanowicz. 2010. Science 2.0 (change will happen ...). *First Monday* 15(7). http://firstmonday.org/htbin/cgiwrap/bin/ojs/index.php/fm/article/view/2961/2573.

Caillois, R. 2001. *Man, Play and Games.* Trans. M. Barash. Urbana, IL: University of Illinois Press.

Carr, N. 2010. *The Shallows: What the Internet Is Doing to Our Brains.* New York: W. W. Norton.

Castells, M. 2000. *The Rise of the Network Society.* Oxford: Blackwell.

Castronova, E. 2005. *Synthetic Worlds: The Business and Culture of Online Games.* Chicago: University of Chicago Press.

Chen, M. G. 2009. Communication, coordination, and camaraderie in World of Warcraft. *Games and Culture* 4 (1): 47–73.

Chen, V. H., and H. B. L. Duh. 2007. Understanding social interaction in World of Warcraft. In *Proceedings of the 4th international conference on advances in computer entertainment technology*, 21–24. New York: Association for Computing Machinery.

Collins, A., and R. Halverson 2009. *Rethinking Education in the Age of Technology: The Digital Revolution and Schooling in America.* The TEC Series. New York: Teachers College Press.

Conner, M. L., and J. G. Clawson, eds. 2009. *Creating a Learning Culture: Strategy, Technology, and Practice.* Cambridge: Cambridge University Press.

Cross, J. 2006. *Informal Learning: Rediscovering the Natural Pathways That Inspire Innovation and Performance.* San Francisco, CA: Pfeiffer.

Csikszentmihalyi, M., and S. Bennett. 1971. An exploratory model of play. *American Anthropologist* 73 (1): 45–58.

Cuenca López, J. M., and M. J. Martín Cáceres. 2010. Virtual games in social science education. *Computers and Education* 55 (3): 1336–1345.

Davidson, C. Forthcoming. *Now You See It: How the Brain Science of Attention Will Change the Ways We Live, Work, and Learn.* New York: Viking Press.

Davidson, C., and D. T. Goldberg. 2009. *The Future of Learning Institutions in a Digital Age.* With the assistance of Z. M. Jones. Cambridge, MA: MIT Press.

———. 2010. *The Future of Thinking: Learning Institutions in a Digital Age.* With the assistance of Z. M. Jones. Cambridge, MA: MIT Press.

Dewey, J. 1991. *The Public and Its Problems.* Athens, OH: Swallow Press.

———. 1997. *Experience and Education.* New York: Touchstone.

———. 2008. *How We Think.* New York: Cosimo Classics.

Dibbell, J. 2006. *Play Money: Or, How I Quit My Day Job and Made Millions Trading Virtual Loot.* New York: Basic Books.

Dijck, J. van. 2009. Users like you? Theorizing agency in user-generated content. *Media Culture Society* 31 (1): 41–58.

Duncan, M. C., G. Chick, and A. Aycock, eds. 1998. *Diversions and Divergences in Fields of Play.* Play and Culture Studies, vol. 1. Greenwich, CT: Ablex Publishing.

Edery, D., and E. Mollick. 2008. *Changing the Game: How Video Games Are Transforming the Future of Business.* Upper Saddle River, NJ: FT Press.

Ellison, N. B., C. Steinfield, and C. Lampe. 2007. The benefits of Facebook "friends": Social capital and college students' use of online social network sites. *Journal of Computer-Mediated Communication* 12 (4): 1143–1168.

Evenson, D. H., and C. E. Hmelo, eds. 2000. *Problem-Based Learning: A Research Perspective on Learning Interactions.* New York: Routledge.

Gardner, H. 1999. *Intelligence Reframed: Multiple Intelligences for the 21st Century.* New York: Basic Books.

———. 2007. *Five Minds for the Future.* Boston: Harvard Business School Press.

Gee, J. P. 2003. *What Video Games Have to Teach Us About Learning and Literacy.* New York: Palgrave Macmillan.

———. 2004. *Situated Language and Learning: A Critique of Traditional Schooling.* New York: Routledge.

———. 2005. *Why Video Games Are Good for Your Soul.* Altona, Australia: Common Ground.

———. 2007a. *Good Video Games and Good Learning: Collected Essays on Video Games, Learning and Literacy.* New Literacies and Digital Epistemologies, vol. 27. New York: Peter Lang.

———. 2007b. Learning and games. In *The Ecology of Games: Connecting Youth, Games, and Learning,* ed. K. Salen, 21–40. John D. and Catherine T. MacArthur

Foundation Series on Digital Media and Learning. Cambridge, MA: MIT Press.

———. 2007c. *What Video Games Have to Teach Us About Learning and Literacy*. 2nd ed. New York: Palgrave Macmillan.

———. 2008. Video games and embodiment. *Games and Culture* 3 (3-4): 253–263.

Gladwell, M. 2002. *The Tipping Point: How Little Things Can Make a Big Difference*. Boston: Back Bay Books.

———. 2008. *Outliers: The Story of Success*. New York: Little, Brown.

Grene, M., ed. 1969. *Knowing and Being: Essays by Michael Polanyi*. Chicago: University of Chicago Press.

Hagel, J., and J. S. Brown. 2005. *The Only Sustainable Edge: Why Business Strategy Depends on Productive Friction and Dynamic Specialization*. Boston: Harvard Business School Press.

Hagel, J., J. S. Brown, and L. Davison. 2010. *The Power of Pull: How Small Moves, Smartly Made, Can Set Big Things in Motion*. New York: Basic Books.

Hayes, E. R., and I. A. Games. 2008. Making computer games and design thinking: A review of current software and strategies. *Games and Culture* 3 (3-4): 309–332.

Herring, S. C. 2004. Slouching toward the ordinary: Current trends in computer-mediated communication. *New Media Society* 6 (1): 26–36.

Hippel, E. von. 2006. *Democratizing Innovation*. Cambridge, MA: MIT Press.

Horvat, E. M., E. B. Weininger, and A. Lareau. 2003. From social ties to social capital: Class differences in the relations between schools and parent networks. *American Educational Research Journal* 40 (2): 319–351.

Huizinga, J. 1971. *Homo Ludens: A Study of the Play-Element in Culture*. Boston: Beacon Press.

Iiyoshi, T., and M. S. Vijay Kumar, eds. 2010. *Opening Up Education: The Collective Advancement of Education through Open Technology, Open Content, and Open Knowledge*. New ed. Cambridge, MA: MIT Press.

Ito, M. 2006. Engineering Play: Children's software and the cultural politics of edutainment. *Discourse* 27 (2): 139–160.

———. 2009. *Engineering Play: A Cultural History of Children's Software*. John D. and Catherine T. MacArthur Foundation Series on Digital Media and Learning. Cambridge, MA: MIT Press.

Ito, M., S. Baumer, M. Bittanti, d. boyd, R. Cody, B. Herr-Stephenson, H. Horst, et al. 2009. *Hanging Out, Messing Around, and Geeking Out: Kids Living and Learning with New Media*. John D. and Catherine T. MacArthur Foundation Series on Digital Media and Learning. Cambridge, MA: MIT Press.

Jenkins, H. 1992. *Textual Poachers: Television Fans and Participatory Culture*. Studies in Culture and Communication. New York: Routledge.

———. 2004. The Cultural Logic of Media Convergence. *International Journal of Cultural Studies* 7 (1): 33–43.

———. 2006a. *Convergence Culture: Where Old and New Media Collide*. Illustr. edn. New York: New York University Press.

———. 2006b. *Fans, Bloggers, and Gamers: Exploring Participatory Culture*. New York: New York University Press.

Johnson, S. 2005. *Everything Bad Is Good for You: How Today's Popular Culture Is Actually Making Us Smarter*. New York: Riverhead Books.

Jones, S. G., ed. 1998. *Cybersociety 2.0: Revisiting Computer-Mediated Community and Technology*. New Media Cultures. Thousand Oaks, CA: Sage Publications.

Juul, J. 2005. *Half-Real: Video Games between Real Rules and Fictional Worlds*.

Cambridge, MA: MIT Press.

Kafai, Y. B. 1995. *Minds in Play: Computer Game Design as a Context for Children's Learning.* [Hillsdale, NJ?]: Lawrence Erlbaum Associates.

———. 2006. Playing and Making Games for Learning: Instructionist and Constructionist Perspectives for Game Studies. *Games and Culture* 1 (1): 36–40.

Kapur, M. Forthcoming. *Productive Failure.* New York: Springer.

Kutner, L., and C. Olson. 2008. *Grand Theft Childhood: The Surprising Truth About Violent Video Games and What Parents Can Do.* New York: Simon and Schuster.

Lareau, A. 2005. *Unequal Childhoods: Class, Race, and Family Life.* Berkeley and Los Angeles: University of California Press.

Laurel, B. 2004. Narrative construction as play. *Interactions* 11 (5): 73–74.

Lave, J. 1996. Teaching, as learning, in practice. *Mind, Culture, and Activity* 3 (3): 149–164.

Lave, J., and E. Wenger. 1991. *Situated Learning: Legitimate Peripheral Participation.* Learning in Doing: Social, Cognitive, and Computational Perspectives. Cambridge: Cambridge University Press.

Lessig, L. 2004. *Free Culture: How Big Media Uses Technology and the Law to Lock Down Culture and Control Creativity.* New York: Penguin Press.

Lim, S. 2009. How and why do college students use Wikipedia? *Journal of the American Society for Information Science and Technology* 60 (11): 2189–2202.

Lytle, D. E., ed. 2003. *Play and Educational Theory and Practice.* Play and Culture Studies, vol. 5. Westport, CT: Praeger.

Malaby, T. 2006. Parlaying value: capital in and beyond virtual worlds. *Games and Culture* 1 (2): 141–162.

Miller, T. 2001. Introducing...cultural citizenship. *Social Text* 19 (4 69): 1–5.

Miller, T., N. Govil, J. McMurria, R. Maxwell, and T. Wang. 2005. *Global Hollywood 2*. London: British Film Institute.

Murray. J. H. 1997. *Hamlet on the Holodeck: The Future of Narrative in Cyberspace*. New York: Free Press.

Nardi, B. 2006. Collaborative play in World of Warcraft. In *LA-WEB '06: Proceedings of the 4th Latin American Web Congress*. Los Alamitos, CA: IEEE Computer Society Press.

Nardi, B. A., S. Ly, and J. Harris. 2007. Learning Conversations in World of Warcraft. In *HICSS '07: Proceedings of the 40th Annual Hawaii International Conference on System Sciences*. Washington, DC: IEEE Computer Society Press.

Nardi, B. A., D. Schiano, M. Gumbrecht, and L. Swartz. 2004. Why we blog. *Communications of the ACM 47* (12): 41–46.

Ondrejka, C. 2004. A piece of place: Modeling the digital on the real in Second Life. Working paper, University of Southern California, Annenberg School for Communication. SSRN: http://ssrn.com/abstract=555883 or doi:10.2139/ssrn.555883.

Palfrey, J., and U. Gasser. 2008. *Born Digital: Understanding the First Generation of Digital Natives*. New York: Basic Books.

Pendleton-Jullian, A. 2009. Design Education and Innovation Ecotones. http://bit.ly/12azD.

———. 2010. *Four (+1) Studios: 7 Papers and an Epilogue*. Charleston, SC: CreateSpace.

Polanyi, M. 1966. *The Tacit Dimension*. Garden City, NY: Doubleday.

Popkewitz, T. S. 1998. Dewey, Vygotsky, and the social administration of the individual: Constructivist pedagogy as systems of ideas in historical spaces. *American Educational Research Journal* 35 (4): 535–570.

Rheingold, H. 2003. *Smart Mobs: The Next Social Revolution.* New York: Basic Books.

Salen, K., and E. Zimmerman. 2003. *Rules of Play: Game Design Fundamentals.* Cambridge, MA: MIT Press.

———, eds. 2005. *The Game Design Reader: A Rules of Play Anthology.* Cambridge, MA: MIT Press.

Seiter, E. 1995. *Sold Separately: Children and Parents in Consumer Culture.* Communications, Media, and Culture. New Brunswick, NJ: Rutgers University Press.

Shirky, C. 2003. Power laws, weblogs, and inequality. *Clay Shirky's Writings About the Internet.* http://shirky.com/writings/powerlaw_weblog.html.

———. 2009. *Here Comes Everybody: The Power of Organizing Without Organizations.* Repr., New York: Penguin.

———. 2010. *Cognitive Surplus: Creativity and Generosity in a Connected Age.* New York: Penguin Press.

Squire, K. 2006. From content to context: Videogames as designed experience. *Educational Researcher* 35 (8): 19–29.

Squire, K., and S. Barab. 2004. Replaying history: engaging urban underserved students in learning world history through computer simulation games. In *ICLS '04: Proceedings of the 6th International Conference of the Learning Sciences,* 505–512. New York: Routledge.

Squire, K. D. 2008. Video game-based learning: An emerging paradigm for instruction. *Performance Improvement Quarterly* 21 (2): 7–36.

Stalder, F. 2006. Manuel Castells: *The Theory of the Network Society*. Key Contemporary Thinkers. Cambridge: Polity Press.

Steinkuehler, C. 2006. The mangle of play. *Games and Culture* 1 (3): 199–213.

Steinkuehler, C., and K. Squire, 2009. Virtual worlds and learning. *On The Horizon*. 17 (1): 8–11.

Steinkuehler, C. A. 2006. Massively multiplayer online video gaming as participation in a discourse. *Mind, Culture, and Activity* 13 (1): 38–52.

Steinkuehler, C. A., and D. Williams. 2006. Where everybody knows your (screen) name: Online games as "third places." *Journal of Computer-Mediated Communication* 11 (4): 885–909.

Sutton-Smith, B. 1997. *The Ambiguity of Play*. Cambridge, MA: Harvard University Press.

Tapscott, D. 1997. *Growing Up Digital: The Rise of the Net Generation*. New York: McGraw-Hill.

Tapscott, D., and A. D. Williams. 2006. *Wikinomics: How Mass Collaboration Changes Everything*. New York: Portfolio.

Taylor, T. L. 2006. *Play Between Worlds: Exploring Online Game Culture*. Cambridge, MA: MIT Press.

Thomas, D. 2003. *Hacker Culture*. Minneapolis, MN: University of Minnesota Press.

Thomas, D., and J. S. Brown. 2007. The play of imagination: Extending the literary mind. *Games and Culture* 2 (2): 149–172.

Turner, M. 1996. *The Literary Mind*. New York: Oxford University Press.

U.S. Department of Education. National Education Technology Plan 2010. www. ed.gov/technology/netp-2010.

Vygotsky, L. S. 1980. *Mind in Society: Development of Higher Psychological Processes.* Eds. M. Cole, V. John-Steiner, S. Scribner, E. Souberman. Cambridge, MA: Harvard University Press.

Wardrip-Fruin, N., and P. Harrigan, eds. 2004. *First Person: New Media as Story, Performance, and Game.* Cambridge, MA: MIT Press.

Wark, M. 2004. *A Hacker Manifesto.* Cambridge, MA: Harvard University Press.

Wartella, E., B. O'Keefe, and R. Scantlin. 2000. Children and Interactive Media: A Compendium of Current Research and Directions for the Future. A report to the Markle Foundation. New York: John and Mary R. Markle Foundation.

Wilkinson, D. M., and B. A. Huberman. 2007. Assessing the value of cooperation in Wikipedia. *First Monday* 12 (4), http://firstmonday.org/htbin/cgiwrap/bin/ojs/index.php/fm/article/view/1763/1643.

Williams, D. 2006. Why Game Studies Now? Gamers Don't Bowl Alone. *Games and Culture* 1 (1): 13–16.

Williams, D., N. Ducheneaut, L. Xiong, Y. Zhang, N. Yee, and E. Nickell. 2006. From tree house to barracks: The social life of guilds in World of Warcraft. *Games and Culture* 1 (4): 338–361.

Wolf, M. J. P. 2002. *The Medium of the Video Game.* Austin, TX: University of Texas Press.

Wolf, M. J. P., and B. Perron, eds. (2003). *The Video Game Theory Reader.* New York: Routledge.

Yee, N. 2006. The labor of fun: How video games blur the boundaries of work and play. *Games and Culture* 1 (1): 68–71.

ACKNOWLEDGEMENTS

We would like to acknowledge several of our colleagues, who consistently steered us in the right direction and generously contributed their time and efforts.

Foremost, we would like to thank Connie Yowell, who founded the John D. and Catherine T. MacArthur Foundation Digital Media and Learning group; Mizuko Ito, who helped nurture it; and the group's members, particularly Diane Rhoten, Katie Salen, Nichole Pinkard, Cathy Davidson, David Goldberg, and danah boyd. We were greatly influenced by them all. We also thank Ernest Wilson, dean of the Annenberg School for Communication, and our friends and colleagues there for their support.

In addition, we have been highly inspired by Ann Pendleton-Jullian and are grateful to her for bringing into our consciousness the role of *homo ludens,* especially as it connects with *homo sapiens* and *homo faber.* We also recognize John Hagel III, of the Deloitte

Center for the Edge, for his leadership in the development of the Shift Index, a framework for defining and measuring the state of change that challenges our old ways of learning.

What's more, we note that this book—especially in its current form—would never have happened without the advice of our agent, James Levine, and his introduction to Lilith Z.C. Fondulas, a phenomenal and patient editor. Paul Soulellis, who designed the book, was also most helpful.

Finally, the authors would like to thank Ann Chisholm and Susan Haviland for their love and encouragement during the writing process.

AUTHORS

DOUGLAS THOMAS is an associate professor at the University of Southern California's Annenberg School for Communication and Journalism. His research focuses on the intersections of technology and culture. It has been funded by the John D. and Catherine T. MacArthur Foundation, the Richard Lounsbery Foundation, and the Annenberg Center for Communication.

Doug is also the author of the book *Hacker Culture* and a coauthor or coeditor of several other books, including *Technological Visions: The Hopes and Fears that Shape New Technologies* and *Cybercrime: Law Enforcement, Security and Surveillance in the Information Age*. He is the founding editor of *Games and Culture: A Journal of Interactive Media,* an international, interdisciplinary journal focused on games research.

JOHN SEELY BROWN is a visiting scholar and an adviser to the provost at the University of Southern California and the independent cochairman of the Deloitte Center for the Edge. He is the author or coauthor of several books, including *The Power of Pull: How Small Moves, Smartly Made, Can Set Big Things in Motion; The Only Sustainable Edge;* and *The Social Life of Information,* which has been translated into nine languages. He has also authored or coauthored more than 100 papers in scientific journals.

Prior to his current position, John was the chief scientist of Xerox and, for nearly two decades, the director of the company's Palo Alto Research Center. He was also a cofounder of the Institute for Research on Learning. He is a member of the American Academy of Arts and Sciences and the National Academy of Education.

A NEW CULTURE OF LEARNING